Bible PROMISES FOR CHAMPIONS

INSPIRATIONS FOR THE YOUNG CHRISTIAN ATHLETE

GARY WILDE

Nashville, Tennessee

Bible Promises for Champions

Nashville, Tennessee 37234

0-8054-9413-8
Dewey Decimal Classification: 242.68
Subject Heading: Athletes

Library of Congress Cataloging-in-Publication Data

Wilde, Gary.
Bible promises for champions / Gary Wilde.
p. cm.
ISBN 0-8054-9413-8 (alk. paper)
1. Athletes--Prayer-books and devotions--English. 2. Sports spectators--Prayer-books and devotions--English. 3. Bible--Quotations. I. Title.

BV4596.A8 W55 2000
242'.68--dc21

99-059712

1 2 3 4 5 04 03 02 01 00
[D]

Introduction

What is a champion?

Is it all about winning? Is it all about how good you are or how many records you break?

No, being a champion is a lot more than won-lost records. Champions are people who make the absolute most of what God has given them, who try their hardest every time they suit up, who leave it all on the field whether it's practice time or game time.

That's what turns an ordinary athlete into a champion.

Sports is one of the ways you prepare for the rest of your life. For real life.

Sometimes you succeed. Sometimes you fail. Just like real life.

Sometimes people support you and cheer you on. Other times you have to put up with trash-talk and put-downs. Just like real life.

Sometimes you get hurt. Sometimes you just want to quit. Sometimes you make a comeback. Just like real life.

But when you're a champion, and when you really do come through—big time—you know it's not just you. A champion knows that nobody can manufacture perfection, not even on the sports field. It's a thing that comes to you, enters your game from out of the blue, free of charge. Sure, you practice and practice, preparing yourself for when it happens to work out like that: when you stroke a high fastball into the left field gap for a two-run, two-out triple, when you sink the winning shot from half court, when you find the strength to charge past the other runners—going uphill. But true champions know that the opportunities to succeed and the ability to make it happen come from God. And from nowhere else. Not even them.

No, not everything that goes into greatness is in our hands alone. We can do all the prep work. But surpassing excellence, especially in real life, is ultimately in Another's hands. A real champion is a guy or girl who knows that this is true, and who lives and plays with thankfulness brimming inside.

Is that you?

I hope this little book will draw you closer to the truth, in sports and in life. I hope that the next time you go out to play, it will help lift your heart in gratitude to God for the miracle of muscles, sweat, leather, grass, ice water, dirt, and sunshine.

Play hard. Give thanks. Be a champ!

—Gary Wilde
Oviedo, Florida
April 2000

Contents

Fear

For God has not given us a spirit of fear, but of power, and of love, and of sound judgment.

—2 Timothy 1:7

Oh, boy. These guys are big.

Huge!

Kids shouldn't be allowed to grow anywhere near that size. Must be the milk. But there they are. Giants, every one of 'em.

Why didn't I stick with the drama club?

C'mon, pull yourself together. You've got a game to play. You've got to get yourself under control.

I just wish it was over.

Jason's not helping my stomach any by staring at me with those big, wide eyes of his during warmups. "We're going down," he says. "I just know it, man. We're going down."

You're Not the First to Face a Giant

And the Philistines stood on a mountain on the one side, and Israel stood on a mountain on the other side, and there was a valley between them.

And there went out a champion out of the camp of the Philistines, named Goliath of Gath, whose height was over nine feet tall.

And he had a helmet of brass upon his head, and he was armed with a coat of mail, and the weight of the coat was five thousand shekels of brass.

And he had greaves of brass upon his legs, and a target of brass between his shoulders.

And the staff of his spear was like a weaver's beam, and his spear's head weighed six hundred shekels of iron, and one bearing a shield went before him. . . .

And the Philistine said, "I defy the armies of Israel this day; give me a man, that we may fight together."

When Saul and all Israel heard those words of the Philistine, they were dismayed, and greatly afraid.

—1 Samuel 17:3-7, 10-11

Let Your Faith Conquer Your Fear

David said to King Saul, "The Lord that delivered me out of the paw of the lion, and out of the paw of the bear will also deliver me out of the hand of this Philistine." And Saul said to David, "Go, and the Lord be with you.". . .

Then David said to the Philistine, "You come to me with a sword, a spear, and a shield, but I come to you in the name of the Lord of hosts, the God of the armies of Israel, whom you have defied.". . .

"And all this assembly will know that the Lord saves not with sword and spear, for the battle is the Lord's, and he will give you into our hands."

And when the Philistine arose and drew near, David ran toward the army to meet the Philistine.

And David put his hand in his bag, took out a stone, and slung it, and hit the Philistine in the forehead so that the stone sunk into his forehead, and he fell on his face to the earth.

So David prevailed over the Philistine with a sling and with a stone, and struck the Philistine and killed him, but there was no sword in the hand of David.

—1 Samuel 17:37, 45, 47-50

Beat Back the Butterflies

"Have I not commanded you? Be strong and of good courage. Don't be afraid or dismayed, for the Lord your God is with you wherever you go."

—Joshua 1:9

"Be strong and of good courage. Fear not or be afraid of them, for the Lord your God, He it is that goes with you. He will not fail you or forsake you."

—Deuteronomy 31:6

Why are you cast down, O my soul, and why are you troubled within me? Hope in God, for I will yet praise Him.

—Psalm 42:5

For I have heard the slander of many. Fear was on every side. While they took counsel together against me, they made plans to take away my life.

—Psalm 31:13

But I will hope continually, and will yet praise You more and more.

—Psalm 71:14

What time I am afraid, I will trust in You.

—Psalm 56:3

These Bible Guys Were Scared, Too

"Fear and trembling came upon me, which made all my bones to shake."

—Job 4:14

And they told Moses, "We came unto the land you sent us, and surely it flows with milk and honey; and this is the fruit of it.

"Nevertheless, the people are strong that dwell in the land, and the cities are walled and very great, and we even saw the children of Anak there."...

And Caleb stilled the people before Moses, and said, "Let us go up at once and possess the land, for we are well able to overcome it."

But the men that went up with him said, "We're not able to go up against the people, for they are stronger than we."...

"We were in our own sight as grasshoppers, and so were we in their sight."

—Numbers 13:27-28, 30-31, 33b

And there came a messenger to David, saying, "The hearts of the men of Israel are after Absalom."

And David said unto all his servants that were with him at Jerusalem, "Arise, and let us flee; for we will not else escape from Absalom. Make speed to depart, lest he overtake us suddenly and bring evil upon us, and strike the city with the edge of the sword."

—2 Samuel 15:13-14

Now as Peter was in the courtyard below, one of the high priest's servants came.

When she saw Peter warming himself, she looked at him and said, "You also were with that Nazarene, Jesus."

But he denied it: "I don't know or understand what you're talking about!" Then he went out to the entryway, and a rooster crowed.

When the servant saw him again, she began to tell those standing nearby, "This man is one of them!"

But again he denied it. After a little while, those standing there said to Peter again, "You certainly are one of them, since you're a Galilean also!"

Then he started to curse and to swear with an oath, "I don't know this man you're talking about!"

—Mark 14:66-71

A Champ's Life Isn't Supposed to Be Easy

"Blessed are those who are persecuted for righteousness, because the kingdom of heaven is theirs.

"Blessed are you when they insult you and persecute you, and say every kind of evil against you falsely because of Me.

"Be glad and rejoice, because your reward is great in heaven. For that is how they persecuted the prophets who were before you."

—Matthew 5:10-12

"I assure you: You will weep and wail, but the world will rejoice. You will become sorrowful, but your sorrow will turn to joy.

"When a woman is in labor she has pain because her time has come. But when she has given birth to a child, she no longer remembers the suffering because of the joy that a person has been born into the world.

"So you also have sorrow now. But I will see you again. Your hearts will rejoice, and no one will rob you of your joy."

—John 16:20-22

"If the world hates you, understand that it hated Me before it hated you.

"If you were of the world, the world would love you as its own. However, because you are not of the world, but I have chosen you out of the world, this is why the world hates you.

"Remember the word I spoke to you: 'A slave is not greater than his master.' If they persecuted Me, they will also persecute you. If they kept My word, they will also keep yours.

"But they will do all these things to you on account of My name, because they don't know the One who sent Me."

—John 15:18-21

"I have told you these things to keep you from stumbling.

"They will ban you from the synagogues. In fact, a time is coming when anyone who kills you will think he is offering service to God.

"They will do these things because they haven't known the Father or Me.

"But I have told you these things so that when their time comes you may remember I told them to you. I didn't tell you these things from the beginning, because I was with you."

—John 16:1-4

"Look: An hour is coming, and has come, when you will be scattered each to his own home, and you will leave Me alone. Yet I am not alone, because the Father is with Me.

"I have told you these things so that in Me you may have peace. In the world you have suffering. But take courage! I have conquered the world."

—John 16:32-33

The Lord will preserve you from all evil.
He will preserve your soul.
The Lord will preserve your going out
and your coming in from this
time forth, and even for evermore.
—Psalm 121:7-8

Don't Be Surprised When Life Gets Hard

My enemies, do not rejoice over me. Though I may fall, I will stand up. Though I may dwell in the dark, the Lord will be my light.

—Micah 7:8

Have Faith and Fight Back

For the weapons of our warfare are not fleshly, but powerful through God for tearing down strongholds, as we tear down arguments.

—2 Corinthians 10:4

Put on all of God's armor so that you can stand against the devil's tactics.

For our battle is not against flesh and blood but against the rulers, against the authorities, against the cosmic powers of this darkness, and against the spiritual forces of the evil one in the heavenly places.

This is why you must take up all of God's armor so you are able to resist in the evil day. And when you have done everything, take your stand.

Stand, therefore, with truth like a belt around your waist, with righteousness like body-armor on your chest.

—Ephesians 6:11-14

But the Lord is faithful, who will strengthen and guard you from the evil one.

—2 Thessalonians 3:3

The Lord will rescue me from every evil work and will save me for His heavenly kingdom. To Him be the glory forever and ever! Amen.

—2 Timothy 4:18

Make Prayer Your First Line of Defense

"As my life was fading away, I remembered the Lord. My prayer came to You, to Your holy temple."

—Jonah 2:7

Behold, the eye of the Lord is upon them that fear Him, upon them that hope in his mercy,

To deliver their soul from death, and to keep them alive in famine.

—Psalm 33:18-19

You will make your prayer unto Him, and He will hear you.

—Job 22:27a

The Lord is my shepherd; I shall not want.

He makes me to lie down in green pastures; He leads me beside the still waters.

He restores my soul; He leads me in the paths of righteousness for His name's sake.

Yes, though I walk through the valley of the shadow of death, I will fear no evil, for You are with me. Your rod and Your staff—they comfort me.

—Psalm 23:1-4

My help comes from the Lord, who made heaven and earth.

He will not suffer your foot to be moved. He that keeps you will not slumber.

—Psalm 121:2-3

Therefore since we have a great High Priest who has passed through the heavens, Jesus, the Son of God, let us hold fast to our confession.

For we do not have a High Priest who is unable to sympathize with our weaknesses, but who has been tempted in all things in quite the same way as we, apart from sin.

Therefore let us approach with joyful hearts to the throne of grace, in order that we may receive mercy and find grace to help in time of need.

—Hebrews 4:14-16

Such is the confidence that we have toward God through Christ.

Not that we are adequate by ourselves to consider anything as coming from ourselves, but our adequacy is from God.

—2 Corinthians 3:4-5

Relax—You're on the Winning Side

For a day in Your courts is better than a thousand. I had rather be a doorkeeper in the house of my God than to dwell in the tents of wickedness.

For the Lord God is a sun and shield. The Lord will give grace and glory. No good thing will He withhold from them that walk uprightly.

O Lord of hosts, blessed is the man that trusts in You.

—Psalm 84:10-12

But there is great gain in godliness with contentment.

For we brought nothing into the world; and so we aren't able to take anything out!

But having food and clothing, with them let us be content.

—1 Timothy 6:6-8

Let your way of life be free from the love of money; be satisfied with your possessions, for He Himself has said: "I will never abandon you nor will I ever forsake you."

—Hebrews 13:5

I don't say this because I am in need, for I have learned to be content in whatever circumstances I am.

I know both how to have little and I know how to have an abundance. In everything and in anything I have learned the secret of both how to be well fed and to have hunger, both to have abundance and to be in need.

—Philippians 4:11-12

I am able to do all things through Him who strengthens me.

—Philippians 4:13

So Are You Ready for Crunch Time?

In fact, when we came into Macedonia, our human nature found no rest, but instead we had trouble at every turn. Outside there were battles; inside there were fears.

But the One who comforts the lowly—that is, God—comforted us.

—2 Corinthians 7:5-6a

Greatly rejoice in this, though now for a season, if need be, your heart is heavy through your many temptations. This trial of your faith, which is much more precious than gold that perishes when it is tried with fire, will show forth praise, honor, and glory at the appearing of Jesus Christ.

—1 Peter 1:6-7

For in the time of trouble, He will hide me in His pavilion. In the secret of His tabernacle, He will hide me; He will set me upon a rock.

—Psalm 27:5

Rejoice in hope; be patient in affliction; be persistent in prayer.

—Romans 12:12

CHECK IT OUT...

Did you know that even the bravest people in the Bible sometimes got afraid? Check these out for yourself.

Abraham—Fearing for his life, he made up a big lie to save his skin. (Genesis 12:10-20)

Moses—God had a big job in store for him, but Moses just had big excuses. (Exodus 4:1-13)

Aaron—He knew that if he stood up for God, the crowd might lay him out. (Exodus 32:15-24)

Elijah—The wicked queen Jezebel wanted him dead, so he headed for the hills. (1 Kings 19:1-10)

Peter—He talked big at first, but lost his courage when it came to crunch time. (Luke 22:54-62)

Courage

The Lord is my light and my salvation; whom shall I fear? The Lord is the strength of my life; of whom shall I be afraid?

—Psalm 27:1

Throw at his head? Are you kidding?

But that's what he said: "Put this one right between his eyes, Bobby. If he can't get outta the way, that's his problem. We're not taking any more of their showing off, you got it?"

But try to hurt somebody?!?
I don't think I should do it.

I mean, he's a substitute coach, just for this game.
Coach Phillips would never tell me to do this.
But then, I want to stay in the game.
I want to stay on the team, too!

You've gotta help me out here, God!
It's time to throw this fastball. . . .

Follow Along on This Real-Life Gut-Check

Through God we will do valiantly, for it is He that will tread down our enemies.

—Psalm 108:13

God Puts Elijah at Odds with a Wicked King

And Elijah the Tishbite, who was of the inhabitants of Gilead, said to Ahab, "As the Lord God of Israel lives, before whom I stand, there will not be dew or rain these years, but according to my word.". . .

And it came to pass after many days that the word of the Lord came to Elijah in the third year, saying, "Go, show yourself unto Ahab; and I will send rain upon the earth."

And Elijah went to show himself unto Ahab. And there was a terrible famine in Samaria. . . .

And it came to pass, when Ahab saw Elijah, that Ahab said unto him, "Are you the one who is troubling Israel?"

And Elijah answered, "I have not troubled Israel, but you and your father's house have, because you have forsaken the commandments of the Lord and you have followed Baalim.

"Now therefore send, and gather to me all Israel unto mount Carmel, and the 450 prophets of Baal and the 400 prophets of the groves which eat at Jezebel's table."

—1 Kings 17:1, 18:1-2, 17-19

Elijah Lays Down the Challenge

So Ahab sent for all the children of Israel and gathered the prophets together at mount Carmel.

And Elijah came unto all the people and said, "How long will you waver between two opinions? If the Lord is

God, follow him, but if Baal is God, then follow him." And the people answered him not a word.

—1 Kings 18:20-21

Let's Get Ready to Rumble

Then Elijah said unto the people, "I, even I only, remain a prophet of the Lord, but Baal's prophets are 450 men.

"Let them therefore give us two bulls. Let them choose one bull for themselves, cut it in pieces, lay it on the wood, and put no fire under it. I will dress the other bull, lay it on the wood, and put no fire under it.

"Then call on the name of your gods, and I will call on the name of the Lord. And the God that answers by fire, let him be God." And all the people answered, "It is well spoken."

And Elijah said unto the prophets of Baal, "Choose you one bull for yourselves and dress it first, for you are many. Call on the name of your gods, but put no fire under it."

—1 Kings 18:22-25

Give It Your Best Shot

And they took the bull which was given them and they dressed it, and called on the name of Baal from morning even until noon, saying, "O Baal, hear us!" But there was no voice, nor any that answered. And they leaped upon the altar which was made.

And it came to pass at noon, that Elijah mocked them, and said, "Cry louder, for he is a god. Either he is talking or pursuing or on a journey. Or perhaps he's asleep and must be awakened."

And they cried aloud and cut themselves after their manner with knives and lances till the blood gushed out upon them.

And when midday was past and they had prophesied until the time of the evening sacrifice, there was neither a voice, nor any to answer, nor any that regarded.

—1 Kings 18:26-29

Now It's My Turn

And Elijah said unto all the people, "Come near unto me." And all the people came near unto him. And he repaired the altar of the Lord that was broken down.

And Elijah took twelve stones, according to the number of the tribes of the sons of Jacob unto whom the word of the Lord came when He said, "Israel will be thy name."

And with the stones, Elijah built an altar in the name of the Lord, and he made a trench around the altar, as great as would contain two measures of seed.

And he put the wood in order, cut the bull in pieces, laid him on the wood, and said, "Fill four barrels with water and pour it on the burnt sacrifice and on the wood."

—1 Kings 18:30-33

I'll Even Give You a Head Start

Then Elijah said, "Do it the second time." And they did it the second time. And he said, "Do it the third time." And they did it the third time.

And the water ran down the altar; and he filled the trench also with water.

And at the time of the evening sacrifice, Elijah the prophet came near and said, "Lord God of Abraham, Isaac, and of Israel, let it be known this day that You are God in Israel, that I am Your servant, and that I have done all these things at Your word.

"Hear me, O Lord, hear me, that these people may

know that You are the Lord God, and that You have turned their hearts back again."

—1 Kings 18:34-37

WATCH WHAT GOD CAN DO

Then the fire of the Lord fell and consumed the burnt sacrifice, the wood, the stones, and the dust, and licked up the water that was in the trench.

And when all the people saw it, they fell on their faces and said, "The Lord, He is God! The Lord, He is God!"

And Elijah said unto them, "Take the prophets of Baal. Let not one of them escape." And they took them, and Elijah brought them down to the brook Kishon and killed them there.

—1 Kings 18:38-40

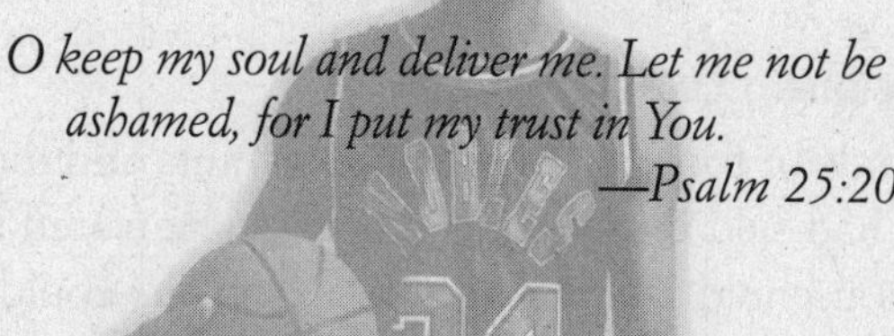

O keep my soul and deliver me. Let me not be ashamed, for I put my trust in You.

—Psalm 25:20

MORE SCENES FROM THE CHAMPIONS HALL OF FAME

And what more shall I say? For the time would fail me if I tell about Gideon, Barak, Samson, Jephthah, both David and Samuel, and the prophets.

These are the ones who, because of their faith, conquered kingdoms, administered justice, obtained promises, shut the mouth of lions, quenched the power of fire, escaped the edge of the sword, were strengthened from weakness, became mighty in battle, turned to flight armies of foreigners.

—Hebrews 11:32-34

King Asa: He Blitzed the Competition

And Asa did what was right in the eyes of the Lord, as did David his father.

And he took away the evildoers out of the land, and removed all the idols that his fathers had made.

He even removed Maachah, his mother, from being queen because she had made an idol in a grove. And Asa destroyed her idol and burned it by the brook Kidron.

But the high places were not removed. Still, Asa's heart was perfect with the Lord all his days.

—1 Kings 15:11-14

Gideon: He Didn't Choke

Then Gideon took ten men of his servants and did as the Lord had said unto him. But because he feared his father's household and the men of the city, he could not do it by day, so he did it by night.

And when the men of the city arose early in the morning, behold, the altar of Baal was cast down, and the grove was cut down that was by it, and the second bull was offered upon the altar that was built.

And they said one to another, "Who has done this thing?" And when they asked, the people said, "Gideon the son of Joash has done this thing."

—Judges 6:27-29

Joshua and Caleb: Come On—We Can Win This One!

And Joshua the son of Nun, and Caleb the son of Jephunneh, which were among those who searched the land, tore their clothes and said unto all the company of the children of Israel, "The land which we passed through to search is an exceeding good land.

"If the Lord delights in us, then He will bring us into this land and give it us—a land which flows with milk and honey.

"But do not rebel against the Lord, neither fear the people of the land, for they are bread for us. Their defense has departed from them, and the Lord is with us. Do not fear them!"

But all the congregation wanted to stone them. Then the glory of the Lord appeared in the tabernacle of the congregation before all the children of Israel.

—Numbers 14:6-10

Jael: The Girl Came Through at Crunch Time

And Jael went out to meet Sisera, and said unto him, "Turn in to me, my lord. Don't be afraid." And when he had turned in unto her into the tent, she covered him with a blanket.

And he said unto her, "Give me, I pray, a little water to drink, for I am thirsty." And she opened a bottle of milk and gave it to him to drink, and covered him.

Again he said unto her, "Stand in the door of the tent, and when any man comes and asks you, 'Is there any man here?' you say, 'No.' "

Then Jael, Heber's wife, took a tent nail and a hammer in her hand, went softly unto him, and drove the nail into his temples, fastening his head to the ground, for he was fast asleep and weary. So he died.

—Judges 4:18-21

THREE HEBREWS: THEY WENT TO THE LINE—PUMPED!

"There are some Jews whom you have appointed over the administration of the province of Babylon: Shadrach, Meshach, and Abednego. These men do not respect you, O king. They do not serve your gods or worship the golden statue that you have set up."

Then Nebuchadnezzar in furious rage gave orders to bring Shadrach, Meshach, and Abednego. So these men were brought before the king.

Shadrach, Meshach, and Abednego replied to the king, "O Nebuchadnezzar, we do not need to offer a defense to you in this matter. . .

"If it happens, our God whom we serve is able to deliver us from the furnace of blazing fire, and He can deliver us from your hand, O king.

"But even if He does not, we want you to know, O king, that we will not serve your gods."

—Daniel 3:12-13, 16-18

NEHEMIAH: NOT GONNA RUN!

Next, I went to the house of Shemaiah, the son of Delaiah, the son of Mehetabel, who, having been confined, said, "Let's meet at the House of God, inside the sanctuary, and shut its doors since they're coming to kill you; indeed, tonight they're coming to kill you!"

Nehemiah responded, "Should a man in my position run away, or could someone in my position even enter the sanctuary to save his life? No, I will not enter!"

Suddenly, I realized and understood that Shemaiah was not sent from God: Tobiah and Sanballat had hired him. Shemaiah had composed the above prophetic word against me.

In fact, he was hired to frighten me into doing what he had suggested so that I would sin, thereby giving them reason to discredit me with a bad name.

—**Nehemiah 6:10-13**

Esther: Do or Die!

Then Mordecai answered Esther, "Do not think that you will escape in the king's house more than all the Jews.

"For if you hold your peace at this time, then deliverance will come to the Jews from another place, but you and your father's house will be destroyed. And who knows whether you have come to the kingdom for such a time as this?"

Then Esther asked them to return this answer to Mordecai, "Go, gather together all the Jews that are present in Shushan and fast for me. Neither eat or drink for three days, night or day. I also and my maidens will fast likewise, and so will I go in unto the king, which is not allowed by the law. And if I perish, I perish."

—**Esther 4:13-16**

Fear does not exist in love. On the contrary, mature love expels fear, because fear involves punishment. But one who is fearful has not been brought to maturity in love.

—1 John 4:18

HEY, YOU CAN DO IT, TOO!

"Listen to me, you that know righteousness, you people who have My law in your hearts: Do not fear the insults of men, neither be afraid of their evil words."

—Isaiah 51:7

When the wicked, even my enemies and my foes came upon me to eat up my flesh, they stumbled and fell.

Though a host should encamp against me, my heart will not fear. Though war should rise against me, I will be confident in this.

—Psalm 27:2-3

The Lord is on my side. I will not fear. What can man do to me?

The Lord takes my part with those who help me. Therefore I will see my desire upon them that hate me.

—Psalm 118:6-7

FACE THE PRESSURE WITH GOD'S POWER

Many are the afflictions of the righteous, but the Lord delivers him out of them all.

—Psalm 34:19

Don't worry about anything, but in everything by prayer and entreaty, let your requests be made known to God with thanksgiving.

Then the peace of God that surpasses all understanding will protect your hearts and your minds in Christ Jesus.

—Philippians 4:6-7

And Israel took his journey with all that he had, came to Beersheba, and offered sacrifices to the God of his father Isaac.

And God spoke to Israel in the visions of the night, and said, "Jacob, Jacob." And he said, "Here I am."

And God said, "I am God, the God of your father. Do not be afraid to go down into Egypt, for I will make of you a great nation there.

"I will go down with you into Egypt, and I will also surely bring you up again. And Joseph will put his hand upon your eyes.

—Genesis 46:1-4

Then the Lord said to Paul in a night vision: "Don't be afraid, but keep on speaking and don't be silent.

"For I am with you, and no one will lay a hand on you to hurt you; because I have many people in this city."

And he stayed there a year and six months, teaching the word of God among them.

—Acts 18:9-11

Already Blown It? God Gives Second Chances

The Lord, your Redeemer, the Holy One of Israel, says, "I am the Lord your God, who teaches you to profit, who leads you by the way that you should go.

"O that you had listened to my commandments! Then your peace would have been as a river, and your righteousness as the waves of the sea."

—Isaiah 48:17-18

"I will also give you a new heart, and a new spirit will I put within you. And I will take away the stony heart out of your flesh, and I will give you a heart of flesh.

"And I will put My spirit within you and cause you to walk in My statutes, and you will keep My judgments and do them."

—**Ezekiel 36:26-27**

We know that all things work together for the good of those who love God: those who are called according to His purpose.

—**Romans 8:28**

"Your heart must not be troubled. Believe in God; believe also in Me.

"In My Father's house are many dwelling places; if not, I would have told you. I am going away to prepare a place for you.

"If I go away and prepare a place for you, I will come back and receive you to Myself, so that where I am you may be also."

—**John 14:1-3**

"I will not leave you as orphans; I am coming to you.

"In a little while the world will see Me no longer, but you will see Me. Because I live, you will live too.

"In that day you will know that I am in My Father, you are in Me, and I am in you."

—**John 14:18-20**

Check It Out...

Take time to read about some other ways God helped His champions be bold and brave.

Joshua—They could keep playing around if they wanted to. He was going with God. (Joshua 24:14-28)

Ruth—Turning her back on everything she knew, she chose the path that led to God. (Ruth 1:8-18)

Daniel—He'd sooner be served up raw to the lions than stop serving the Lord. (Daniel 6:10-23)

Stephen—He was more willing to die at the hand of a cruel mob than to deny his faith. (Acts 7:51-60)

Paul—Knowing that trouble awaited him everywhere he went, he went ahead anyway. (Acts 20:22-32)

Pain

So then I am satisfied with weaknesses, with mistreatments, with distress, with persecutions, with stressful situations because of Christ. For whenever I am weak, then I am strong.

—2 Corinthians 12:10

Tape the right ankle. Tape the left ankle. Then the knee. Buckle on that crazy brace contraption. Get weighted down with steel and straps and a bunch of worn-out velcro.

So how am I supposed to move, let alone chase a volleyball?

After practice: round two. Two ice packs—at least. *Gotta keep the swelling down, Sarah*. I know, I know.

The trip home. The temptation to overdose on ibuprofen. Try to concentrate on homework. *Is it really almost midnight already?*

The other girls don't seem to suffer so much. Why me? Why am I always the one getting hurt? *Is it worth it?*

But there's nothing like a slap-bang, flaming spike. Nothing like it in the world.

PAIN IS A PART OF THE GAME

Dear friends, don't think the fiery trial which is trying you is strange, as though some unusual thing is happening to you.

But rejoice, seeing as you are partakers of Christ's sufferings, so that when His glory is revealed, you may be glad also with exceeding joy.

—1 Peter 4:12-13

Now all discipline for the present does not seem to be a matter of joy but of grief; but later it yields the peaceful fruit of righteousness to those who have been trained through it.

—Hebrews 12:11

For our slight momentary trouble is accomplishing for us a superlatively abundant eternal weight of glory, because we focus not on what is seen, but on what is unseen; for what is seen is temporal, but what is unseen is eternal.

—2 Corinthians 4:17-18

For I consider that the sufferings of this present time are not worth comparing with the glory that is going to be revealed to us.

—Romans 8:18

This saying is trustworthy: For if we die with Him We will also live with Him.

If we endure, we will also reign with Him. If we deny Him He will also deny us.

—2 Timothy 2:11-12

But the God of all grace, who has called us to his eternal glory by Christ Jesus, will, after you have suffered a little while, make you perfect—establish, strengthen, and settle you.

—1 Peter 5:10

Finally, be strong in the Lord and in His vast strength.

—Ephesians 6:10

Remember Jesus: He's Been There, Done That

But the One who for a short time has been made lower than angels we see—Jesus—because of the suffering of death crowned with glory and honor, that by God's grace He might taste death on behalf of all.

—Hebrews 2:9

An Innocent Man, Sentenced to Death

Then He withdrew from them about a stone's throw, knelt down, and began to pray, "Father, if You are willing, take this cup away from Me—nevertheless, not My will, but Yours, be done."

Then an angel from heaven appeared to Him, strengthening Him.

Being in anguish, He prayed more fervently, and His sweat became like drops of blood falling to the ground.

—Luke 22:41-44

While He was still speaking, Judas, one of the Twelve, suddenly arrived. With him was a large mob, with swords and clubs, who were sent by the chief priests and elders of the people.

His betrayer had given them a sign: "The one I kiss, He's the one; arrest Him!"

So he went right up to Jesus and said, "Greetings, Rabbi!"—and kissed Him.

"Friend," Jesus asked him, "why have you come?" Then they came up, took hold of Jesus, and arrested Him.

—Matthew 26:47-50

At that time Jesus said to the crowds, "Have you come out with swords and clubs, as if I were a criminal, to capture Me? Every day I used to sit, teaching in the temple complex, and you didn't arrest Me.

"But all this has happened so that the prophetic Scriptures would be fulfilled." Then all the disciples deserted Him and ran away.

—Matthew 26:55-56

You Call This Fair?

The chief priests and the whole Sanhedrin were looking for false testimony against Jesus so they could put Him to death.

But they could not find any, even though many false witnesses came forward. Finally, two who came forward stated, "This man said, 'I can demolish God's sanctuary and rebuild it in three days.' "

The high priest then stood up and said to Him, "Don't You have an answer to what these men are testifying against You?"

But Jesus kept silent. Then the high priest said to Him, "By the living God I place You under oath: tell us if You are the Messiah, the Son of God!"

"You have said it yourself," Jesus told him. "But I tell you, in the future you will see 'the Son of Man seated at the right hand' of the Power, and 'coming on the clouds of heaven.' "

—Matthew 26:59-64

Then the high priest tore his robes and said, "He has blasphemed! Why do we still need witnesses? Look, now you've heard the blasphemy! What is your decision?"

They answered, "He deserves death!"

Then they spit in His face and beat Him; and others slapped Him and said, "Prophesy to us, you Messiah! Who hit You?"

—Matthew 26:65-68

Now Jesus stood before the governor. "Are You the King of the Jews?" the governor asked Him. Jesus answered, "You have said it yourself."

And while He was being accused by the chief priests and elders, He didn't answer.

Then Pilate said to Him, "Don't You hear how much they are testifying against You?"

But He didn't answer him on even one charge, so that the governor was greatly amazed.

—Matthew 27:11-14

Pilate asked them, "What should I do then with Jesus, who is called Messiah?" They all answered, "Crucify Him!"

Then he said, "Why? What has He done wrong?" But they kept shouting, "Crucify Him!" all the more.

When Pilate saw that he was getting nowhere, but that a riot was starting instead, he took some water, washed his hands in front of the crowd, and said, "I am innocent of this man's blood. See to it yourselves!"

All the people answered, "His blood be on us and on our children!"

Then he released Barabbas to them. But after having Jesus flogged, he handed Him over to be crucified.

—Matthew 27:22-26

Jesus Was Tortured

Then the governor's soldiers took Jesus into headquarters and gathered the whole company around Him.

They stripped Him and dressed Him in a scarlet robe.

They twisted a crown out of thorns, put it on His head, and placed a reed in His right hand. And they knelt down before Him and mocked Him: "Hail, King of the Jews!"

Then they spit at Him, took the reed, and kept hitting Him on the head.

When they had mocked Him, they stripped Him of the robe, put His clothes on Him, and led Him away to crucify Him.

—Matthew 27:27-31

They Nailed Him Hand and Foot to the Cross

As they led Him away, they seized Simon, a Cyrenian, who was coming in from the country, and laid the cross on him to carry behind Jesus.

A great multitude of the people followed Him, including women who were mourning and lamenting Him.

—Luke 23:26-27

And they brought Him to the place called Golgotha (which means Skull Place).

They tried to give Him wine mixed with myrrh, but He

did not take it.

Then they crucified Him and divided His clothes by casting lots for them to decide what each would get.

Now it was nine in the morning when they crucified Him.

The inscription of the charge written against Him was: THE KING OF THE JEWS.

—Mark 15:22-26

It was now about noon, and darkness came over the whole land until three, because the sun's light failed. The curtain of the sanctuary was split down the middle.

And Jesus called out with a loud voice, "Father, into Your hands I entrust My spirit." Saying this, He breathed His last.

When the centurion saw what happened, he began to glorify God, saying, "This man really was righteous!"

All the crowds that had gathered for this spectacle, when they saw what had taken place, went home, striking their chests.

—Luke 23:44-48

But Jesus Made the Ultimate Comeback!

After the Sabbath, as the first day of the week was dawning, Mary Magdalene and the other Mary went to view the tomb.

Suddenly there was a violent earthquake, because an angel of the Lord descended from heaven and approached the tomb. He rolled back the stone and was sitting on it.

His appearance was like lightning, and his robe was as white as snow.

The guards were so shaken from fear of him that they became like dead men.

—Matthew 28:1-4

So the women were terrified and bowed down to the ground. "Why are you looking for the living among the dead?" asked the men.

"He is not here, but He has been resurrected! Remember how He spoke to you when He was still in Galilee, saying, 'The Son of Man must be betrayed into the hands of sinful men, be crucified, and rise on the third day'?"

And they remembered His words.

—Luke 24:5-8

Returning from the tomb, they reported all these things to the Eleven and to all the rest.

Mary Magdalene, Joanna, Mary the mother of James, and the other women with them were telling the apostles these things.

But these words seemed like nonsense to them, and they did not believe the women.

Peter, however, got up and ran to the tomb. When he stooped to look in, he saw only the linen cloths. So he went home, amazed at what had happened.

—Luke 24:9-12

In the evening of that first day of the week, the disciples were gathered together with the doors locked because of their fear of the Jews. Then Jesus came, stood among them, and said to them, "Peace to you!"

Having said this, He showed them His hands and His side. So the disciples rejoiced when they saw the Lord.

Jesus said to them again, "Peace to you! Just as the Father has sent Me, I also send you."

—John 20:19-21

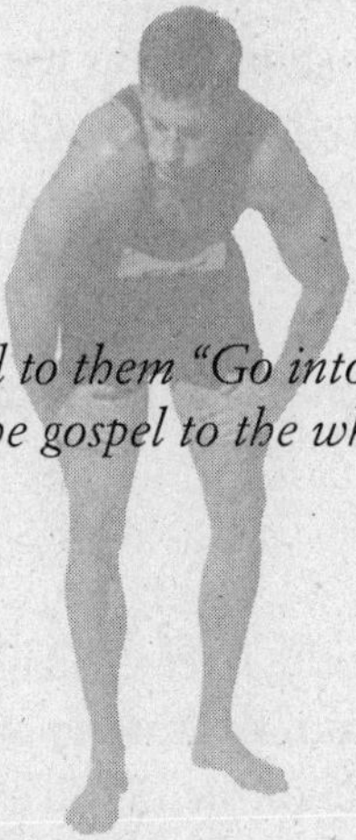

Then He said to them "Go into all the world and preach the gospel to the whole creation."
—Mark 16:15

HE PAVED OUR WAY TO HEAVEN

After He had said this, while they were watching, He was taken up, and a cloud received Him out of their sight.

While they were gazing into heaven as He was going, suddenly two men stood by them in white clothes, who also said, "Men of Galilee, why do you stand looking up into heaven? This Jesus, who has been taken up from you into heaven, will come in the same way as you have seen Him going into heaven."

—Acts 1:9-11

"Look! I am coming quickly, and My reward is with Me to repay each person according to what he has done.

"I am the Alpha and the Omega, the First and the Last, the Beginning and the End.

"Blessed are those who wash their robes, so that they may have the right to the tree of life and may enter the city by the gates."

—Revelation 22:12-14

Crown Him the Champion!

And He put everything under His feet and appointed Him head over everything in the church, which is His body, the fullness of the One who fills all things in every way.

—Ephesians 1:22-23

For He must reign until He has put all enemies under His feet.

—1 Corinthians 15:25

Then he showed me the river of living water, sparkling like crystal, flowing from the throne of God and of the Lamb down the middle of the broad street of the city.

On both sides of the river was the tree of life bearing twelve kinds of fruit, producing its fruit every month. The leaves of the tree are for healing the nations, and there will no longer be any curse. The throne of God and of the Lamb will be in the city, and His servants will serve Him.

They will see His face, and His name will be on their foreheads.

Night will no longer exist, and people will not need lamplight or sunlight, because the Lord God will give them light. And they will reign forever and ever.

—Revelation 22:1-5

Pay the Price, Live the Life

As every man has received the gift, even so minister the same one to another, as good stewards of the manifold grace of God.

If any man speaks, let him speak as the oracles of God. If any man ministers, let him do it with the ability which God gives, so that God in all things may be glorified through

Jesus Christ, to whom be praise and dominion forever and ever. Amen.

—1 Peter 4:10-11

Have this attitude among you which was also in Christ Jesus:

Who, although He existed in the form of God, did not consider equality with God as something to be grasped.

Instead, He emptied Himself by taking the form of a slave, by being made in the likeness of men.

And being found in appearance as a man, He humbled Himself by becoming obedient to the point of death — even death on a cross.

For this reason God also highly exalted Him, and bestowed on Him the name above every name; so that at the name of Jesus, every knee should bend in heaven and on earth and under the earth, and every tongue confess that Jesus Christ is Lord, to the glory of God the Father.

—Philippians 2:5-11

He is the image of the invisible God, the firstborn of all creation; because by Him everything in heaven and on earth were created, things visible and invisible, whether thrones or dominions or rulers or powers—all things have been created through Him and for Him.

And He Himself is before all things, and in Him all things hold together.

He is also the head of the body, the church; He is the beginning, the firstborn from the dead, so that He might come to have first place in everything.

Because in Him all the fullness of God was pleased to dwell.

—Colossians 1:15-19

If you are reproached for the name of Christ, happy are you, for the spirit of glory and of God rests upon you. On their part He is evil spoken of, but on your part He is glorified.

But let none of you suffer as a murderer, a thief, an evildoer, or a busybody in other men's matters.

Yet if any man suffer as a Christian, let him not be ashamed, but let him glorify God on this behalf.

—1 Peter 4:14-16

"I assure you: The one who believes in Me will also do the works that I do. And he will do even greater works than these, because I am going to the Father."

—John 14:12

Check It Out...

Pain is plentiful in the Bible—and in life. But help is always on the way. Read on and see.

Hannah—A sad wife longing for a child, she found a God who answers prayers. (1 Samuel 1:9-18)

Shunemite Woman—She wouldn't sit quietly and let her son die a useless death. (2 Kings 4:18-37)

Job—He literally lost everything he had, but he hung in there to the better end. (Job 42:9-17)

Sick Woman—After years of suffering, she found help in one moment with Jesus. (Mark 5:25-34)

Thief on the cross—In his last gasp before death, he turned to Jesus and found life. (Luke 23:32-43)

Power

"For by You I have run through a troop; by my God I have leaped over a wall."

—2 Samuel 22:30

You can't hit a baseball with any power at all. You couldn't throw a spiral if your life depended on it. You don't even run very fast.

But I can jump—always could.

Now it's time to show what the springs in those legs can do. The bar moves a couple inches higher. The team's a couple points down. If track and field means anything, it means coming through under pressure. And this time, it boils down to you and those legs.

Are they going to do it for me this time?

Nobody else can help. No one else can run down that lane for you, take those final steps—one…two…three… and then launch into the sky. You're flying high. You're as light as a feather. Gravity waits and wonders.

Can I do it, when it's all on the line?

Sometimes, You Feel Like You've Got Nothing

"If you have run with the footmen and they have wearied you, then how can you contend with horses?"

—Jeremiah 12:5a

"Flight will be lost to the swift, the strong man will not succeed by his strength, and the warrior will not save his life."

—Amos 2:14

"And they will fall one upon another as if before a sword when no one is pursuing them, and you will have no power to stand before your enemies."

—Leviticus 26:37

Is there no balm in Gilead? Is there no physician there? Why then is the health of the daughter of my people not recovered?

—Jeremiah 8:22

Where's Your Source of Strength?

"O our God, will You not judge them? For we have no might against this great company that comes against us, neither do we know what to do. But our eyes are upon You."

—2 Chronicles 20:12

"Behold, God is mighty and despises not any. He is mighty in strength and wisdom."

—Job 36:5

Behold, the Lord rides upon a swift cloud and will come into Egypt. The idols of Egypt will be moved at his presence, and the heart of Egypt will melt in the midst of it.

—Isaiah 19:1

He does not delight in the strength of the horse; He takes no pleasure in the legs of a man.

The Lord takes pleasure in those that fear Him, in those that hope in His mercy.

—Psalm 147:10-11

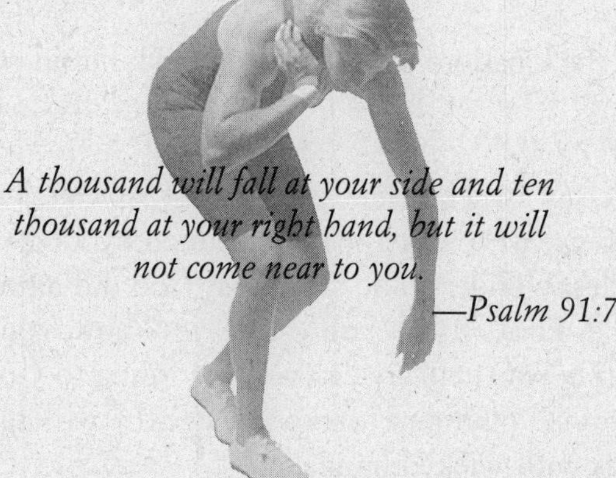

A thousand will fall at your side and ten thousand at your right hand, but it will not come near to you.

—Psalm 91:7

Because you have made the Lord, who is my refuge, even the most High your habitation, no evil will befall you, neither will any plague come near your dwelling.

—Psalm 91:9-10

And Asa cried unto the Lord his God, "Lord, it is nothing with You to help, whether with many or with those that have no power. Help us, O Lord our God, for we rest on You, and in Your name we go against this multitude. O Lord, You are our God; don't let man prevail against You."

—2 Chronicles 14:11

No king is saved by the multitude of a host; a mighty man is not delivered by much strength.

—Psalm 33:16

There's No Maybe in God's Might

There is no one like You, O Lord. You are great, and Your name is great in might.

—Jeremiah 10:6

For the kingdom of God is not in talk but in power.

—1 Corinthians 4:20

"Men of Israel, listen to these words: This Jesus the Nazarene, who was a man accredited by God to you by miracles, wonders, and signs that God did among you through Him, just as you yourselves know, you killed, when He was delivered to you according to God's determined plan and foreknowledge, by nailing Him to a cross with wicked hands.

"God raised Him up, having brought the pangs of death to an end, because it was impossible for Him to be held by death."

—Acts 2:22-24

And they were astonished at His teaching because His message had authority.

—Luke 4:32

Gotta Plant Those Feet

"He will keep the feet of his saints, and the wicked will be silent in darkness, for no man will prevail by strength."

—1 Samuel 2:9

For the Lord will be your confidence and will keep your foot from a snare.

—Proverbs 3:26

I thought on my ways, and turned my feet unto Your testimonies.

—Psalm 119:59

Your word is a lamp unto my feet and a light unto my path.

—Psalm 119:105

Pay attention to the habitual paths of your feet, and all your ways will be certain.

—Proverbs 4:26

Then you will go in your way with confidence, and your foot will not stumble.

—Proverbs 3:23

It's Not Your Size, But Your Spirit

"A little one will become a thousand, and a small one a strong nation. I the Lord will hasten it in its time."

—Isaiah 60:22

And He said to me, "My grace is sufficient for you, for My power is perfected in weakness." Most gladly, therefore, I will boast instead in my weaknesses, so that the power of Christ may rest on me.

—2 Corinthians 12:9

For consider your calling, brothers: Not many wise, humanly speaking, not many mighty, not many noble, are called.

But God has chosen the world's stupid things to shame the wise, and God has chosen the world's weak things to shame the mighty things.

And God has chosen the world's base things and the things which are despised, the things that do not exist, to put the things that exist out of commission.

—1 Corinthians 1:26-28

I pray that the eyes of your heart may be enlightened so you may know what is the hope of His calling, what are the riches of the glory of His inheritance in the saints, and what is the immeasurable greatness of His power to us who believe according to the working of His vast strength.

He demonstrated this power in the Messiah by raising Him from the dead and seating Him at His right hand in the heavenly places.

—Ephesians 1:18-20

Now we have this treasure in jars of clay, in order that the excellence of the power may be ascribed to God and not to us.

—2 Corinthians 4:7

You are kept by the power of God through faith unto salvation ready to be revealed in the last time.

—1 Peter 1:5

This Is His Battle, Not Yours

And he said, "Listen, all Judah, inhabitants of Jerusalem, and king Jehoshaphat: Thus says the Lord to you, 'Do not be afraid or dismayed because of this great multitude, for the battle is not yours, but God's. . . .

" 'You will not need to fight in this battle. Set yourselves, stand still, and see the salvation of the Lord with you, O Judah and Jerusalem.' Don't be afraid or dismayed. Tomorrow go out against them, for the Lord will be with you."

—2 Chronicles 20:15, 17

"The one who believes in Me, as the Scripture has said, will have streams of living water flow from deep within him."

He said this about the Spirit, whom those who believed in Him were going to receive, for the Spirit had not yet been received, because Jesus had not yet been glorified.

—John 7:38-39

"And look, I am sending you what My Father promised. As for you, stay in the city until you are empowered from on high."

—Luke 24:49

"But you will receive power when the Holy Spirit has come upon you; and you will be My witnesses in Jerusalem, in all Judea and Samaria, and to the ends of the earth."

—Acts 1:8

"Look, I have given you the authority to trample on snakes and scorpions and over all the power of the enemy; nothing will ever harm you."

—Luke 10:19

"So when they arrest you and hand you over, don't worry beforehand what you will say. On the contrary, whatever is given to you in that hour—say it. For it isn't you who are speaking, but the Holy Spirit."

—Mark 13:11

Put Your Confidence in a Safe Place

"And he will go before Him in the spirit and power of Elijah, to turn the hearts of fathers to their children and the disobedient to the understanding of the righteous, to make ready for the Lord a prepared people."

—Luke 1:17

It is better to trust in the Lord than to put confidence in man.
It is better to trust in the Lord than to put confidence in princes.

—Psalm 118:8-9

For to me, to live is Christ and to die is gain.

—Philippians 1:21

I have been crucified with Christ: it is no longer I who live, but Christ lives in me; and the life which I now live in the flesh, I live by faith in the Son of God, who loved me and offered Himself up for me.

—Galatians 2:20

Fellow believers, if our heart does not condemn us, we have boldness towards God.

—1 John 3:21

For we have been made sharers of Christ, if we just retain faithfully to the end the beginning of our confidence.

—Hebrews 3:14

Don't Be Like These Unwise Guys

And they said, "Come, let us build a city and a tower whose top may reach to heaven, and let us make us a name, lest we be scattered abroad upon the face of the whole earth.". . .

So the Lord scattered them abroad from there upon the face of all the earth, and they stopped building the city.

—Genesis 11:4, 8

And Samuel said to Saul, "You have done foolishly. You have not kept the commandment of the Lord your God which he commanded you. If you had, the Lord would have established your kingdom in Israel for ever.

"But now your kingdom will not continue. The Lord has sought a man after His own heart, and the Lord has commanded him to be captain over His people, because you have not kept that which the Lord commanded you."

—1 Samuel 13:13-14

And at that time Hanani the seer came to Asa king of Judah and said to him, "Because you have relied on the king of Syria and not on the Lord your God, the host of the king of Syria escaped out of your hand.

"Were not the Ethiopians and the Libyans a huge host with very many chariots and horsemen? Yet because you relied on the Lord, he delivered them into your hand.

"For the eyes of the Lord run to and fro throughout the whole earth to show Himself strong on behalf of those whose hearts are perfect toward Him. You have done foolishly in this; therefore, from now on you will have wars."

—2 Chronicles 16:7-9

You also made a ditch between the two walls for the water of the old pool, but you did not look to the maker of it, neither did you have respect for him that fashioned it long ago.

—Isaiah 22:11

So Jonah got up to run away from the Lord's presence to Tarshish. He went down to Joppa and found a ship going to Tarshish. He paid the fare and went down into it to go with them to Tarshish away from the Lord's presence.

But the Lord hurled a violent wind onto the sea, and such a violent storm came upon the sea that the ship threatened to break apart.

The sailors were afraid and cried out each to his god, and they hurled the ship's equipment and cargo into the sea to lighten the load. Meanwhile, Jonah had gone down into the lowest part of the vessel, stretched out, and fallen into a deep sleep.

—Jonah 1:3-5

Come to the True Power Source

"I am the vine; you are the branches. The one who remains in Me and I in him produces much fruit, because you can do nothing without Me."

—John 15:5

Peter told Him, "Even if everyone falls because of You, I will never fall!"

—Matthew 26:33

"Though He slay me, yet will I trust in Him."

—Job 13:15a

From that moment many of His disciples turned back and no longer walked with Him.

Therefore Jesus said to the Twelve, "You don't want to go away too, do you?"

Simon Peter answered, "Lord, to whom should we go? You have the words of eternal life. And we have come to believe and know that You are the Holy One of God!"

—John 6:66-69

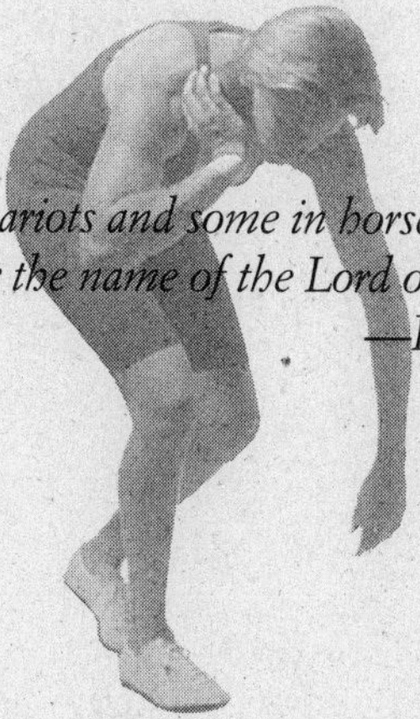

Some trust in chariots and some in horses, but we will remember the name of the Lord our God.

—Psalm 20:7

CHECK IT OUT...

God's power goes way back—to stories like these— and to people like you.

Israelite Army—They knew God was powerful, but could He make time stand still? (Joshua 10:7-14)

Samson—He'd messed up bad along the way, but God was with him to the end. (Judges 16:21-31)

Isaiah—He was just an ordinary guy, but he found that he served an extraordinary God. (Isaiah 6:1-8)

Apostles—They had a lot more power going for them than met the eye. (Matthew 10:16-28)

Paul & Silas—The jailhouse was rocking and rolling when God got through with it. (Acts 16:19-32)

Rules

If anyone competes in sports, he is not crowned unless he competes according to the rules.

—2 Timothy 2:5

"C'mon, who's going to know whether you stick to the course once you get into those woods? I checked it out! My little 'detour' cuts off about 20 yards. All we have to do is be far enough ahead once we top that hill."

My friend Chris doesn't usually invite me to cheat. But then, she's all-out competitive when it comes to her cross-country races.

Now I'm wondering whether all of her wins really mean anything.

But Chris, that's breaking the rules—even if nobody notices.

"Hey, rules were made to be broken, right? Isn't that what they always say?"

Rules Were Made to Be Obeyed

Now by this we know that we have come to know Him: If we keep His commands.

—1 John 2:3

For whoever keeps the entire law, yet fails in one thing, is guilty in all things.

—James 2:10

"Don't assume that I came to destroy the Law or the Prophets. I did not come to destroy but to fulfill.

"For I assure you: Until heaven and earth pass away, not the smallest letter or one stroke of a letter will ever pass from the law until all things are accomplished.

"Therefore, whoever breaks one of the least of these commandments and teaches people to do so, will be called least in the kingdom of heaven. But whoever practices and teaches these commandments will be called great in the kingdom of heaven.

"For I tell you, unless your righteousness surpasses that of the scribes and Pharisees, you will never enter the kingdom of heaven."

—Matthew 5:17-20

The Way You Play Proves Whose Side You're On

Do not love the world or the things in the world. If anyone loves the world, the love of the Father is not in him. Because everything in the world—the lust of the flesh, the lust of the eyes and the pompous pride of life—is not from the Father, but is from the world.

And the world is passing away, and its lust, but whoever does God's will remains forever.

—1 John 2:15-17

Do not be conformed to this age, but be transformed by the renewing of your mind, so that you may discern what is the good, pleasing, and perfect will of God.

—Romans 12:2

Do you not know that friendship with the world is enmity against God? So whoever wants to be the world's friend becomes an enemy of God.

—James 4:4

So if you have been raised with Christ, seek the things that are above, where Christ is, seated at the right hand of God.

Set your minds on things that are above, not on things that are on earth.

—Colossians 3:1-2

Have You Read The Original Rulebook Lately?

Then God spoke all these words, saying:

—Exodus 20:1

The First Commandment

"I am the Lord your God, who has brought you out of the land of Egypt, out of the house of bondage.

"You shall have no other gods before Me."

—Exodus 20:2-3

The Second Commandment

"You shall not make unto you any graven image or any likeness of anything that is in heaven above, in the earth beneath, or in the water under the earth.

"You shall not bow down to them or serve them, for I the Lord your God am a jealous God, visiting the iniquity of the fathers upon the children unto the third and fourth generation of those who hate Me, and showing mercy unto thousands of those who love Me and keep My commandments."

—Exodus 20:4-6

The Third Commandment

"You shall not take the name of the Lord your God in vain, for the Lord will not hold him guiltless who takes His name in vain."

—Exodus 20:7

The Fourth Commandment

"Remember the sabbath day, to keep it holy.

"Six days you shall labor and do all your work, but the seventh day is the sabbath of the Lord your God. You shall not do any work in it—you, your son, your daughter, your manservant, your maidservant, your cattle, or the stranger that is within your gates.

"For in six days the Lord made heaven and earth—the sea and all that is in them—and rested the seventh day. Therefore the Lord blessed the sabbath day and hallowed it."

—Exodus 20:8-11

The Fifth Commandment

"Honor your father and your mother, that your days may be long in the land which the Lord your God gives you."

—Exodus 20:12

The Sixth Commandment

"You shall not kill."

—Exodus 20:13

The Seventh Commandment

"You shall not commit adultery."

—Exodus 20:14

The Eighth Commandment

"You shall not steal."

—Exodus 20:15

The Ninth Commandment

"You shall not bear false witness against your neighbor."

—Exodus 20:16

The Tenth Commandment

"You shall not covet your neighbor's house, your neighbor's wife, his manservant, his maidservant, his ox, his donkey, or anything that is your neighbor's."

—Exodus 20:17

Jesus Turned the Ten into Two

"Teacher, which commandment in the law is the greatest?"

He said to him, " 'You shall love the Lord your God with all your heart, with all your soul, and with all your mind.'

"This is the greatest and most important commandment.

"The second is like it: 'You shall love your neighbor as yourself.' "

—Matthew 22:36-39

"There is no other commandment greater than these."

—Mark 12:31b

The commandments: You shall not commit adultery, You shall not murder, You shall not steal, You shall not covet—and if there is any other commandment, everything is summed up by this: "You shall love your neighbor as yourself."

Love does no wrong to a neighbor. Love, therefore, is the fulfillment of the law.

—Romans 13:9-10

Jesus Turned Up the Heat, Too

"You have heard that it was said to our ancestors, 'You shall not murder,' and 'whoever murders will be subject to judgment.'

"But I tell you, everyone who is angry with his brother will be subject to judgment. And whoever says to his brother, 'Fool!' will be subject to the council. But whoever says, 'You moron!' will be subject to hellfire."

—Matthew 5:21-22

"So if you are offering your gift on the altar, and there you remember that your brother has something against you, leave your gift there in front of the altar. First go and be reconciled with your brother, and then come and offer your gift."

—**Matthew 5:23-24**

"You have heard that it was said, 'You shall not commit adultery.'

"But I tell you, everyone who looks at a woman to lust for her has already committed adultery with her in his heart."

—**Matthew 5:27-28**

"Again, you have heard that it was said to our ancestors, 'You must not break your oath, but you must keep your oaths to the Lord.'

"But I tell you, don't take an oath at all: either by heaven, because it is God's throne; or by the earth, because it is His footstool; or by Jerusalem, because it is the city of the great King.

"Neither should you swear by your head, because you cannot make a single hair white or black.

"But let your word 'yes,' be 'yes,' and your 'no,' be 'no!' Anything more than this is from the evil one."

—**Matthew 5:33-37**

"You have heard that it was said, 'You shall love your neighbor and hate your enemy.'

"But I tell you, love your enemies, and pray for those who persecute you, so that you may be sons of your Father in heaven.

"For He causes His sun to rise on the evil and the good, and sends rain on the righteous and the unrighteous."

—Matthew 5:43-45

"For if you love those who love you, what reward will you have? Don't even the tax collectors do the same? And if you greet only your brothers, what are you doing out of the ordinary? Don't even the Gentiles do the same?"

—Matthew 5:46-47

"Be perfect, therefore, as your Heavenly Father is perfect."

—Matthew 5:48

Ever Feel Like Taking a Short Cut?

"My soul is weary of my life. I will leave my complaint upon myself. I will speak in the bitterness of my soul."

—Job 10:1

"Rather, they refused to obey, failing to remember your wonders that you had performed in their midst, and, in their rebellion, appointed a leader to return them to their slavery. You, however, are a God of forgiveness, gracious and compassionate, slow to anger and abounding in covenant faithfulness. You didn't forsake them!"

—Nehemiah 9:17

Be angry but do not sin. Don't let the sun go down on your wrath.

—Ephesians 4:26

Stand in awe, and do not sin. Commune with your own heart on your bed, and be still.

—Psalm 4:4

All bitterness, anger and wrath, insult and slander must be removed from you, including all wickedness.
—Ephesians 4:31

As you do so, watch with constant care lest there should be anyone who falls back from the grace of God; lest any root of bitterness should spring up and cause trouble, and by this means many be defiled.

—Hebrews 12:15

There's a Right Way and a Wrong Way

The conclusion of the matter, when all has been heard is: fear God and keep his commandments, for this is for all humanity, because God will bring all deeds into judgment, including every hidden thing, whether good or evil.

—Ecclesiastes 12:13-14

Therefore we must so much the more pay attention to the things we have heard, so that we do not drift away. For if the message spoken through angels was reliable, and every transgression and disobedience received a just penalty, how will we escape, if we neglect such a great salvation?

—Hebrews 2:1-3a

So they called for them and ordered them not to preach or teach at all in the name of Jesus.

But Peter and John answered them, "Whether it's right in the sight of God to listen to you rather than to Him, you be the judge.

"But we are unable to stop speaking about what we have seen and heard."

—Acts 4:18-20

Wherefore then we also, since we have so great a cloud of witnesses surrounding us, let us lay aside every encumbrance and the easily ensnaring sin, and with endurance let us run the race lying before us.

—Hebrews 12:1

Choose the Right Way

"You are My friends, if you do what I command you."

—John 15:14

Everyone who believes that Jesus is the Messiah has been born of God, and everyone who loves the parent also loves his offspring.

By this we know that we love God's children, whenever we love God and obey His commands.

For this is the love of God, that we keep His commands, and His commands are not a burden.

—1 John 5:1-3

But someone will say: "You have faith, and I have works." Show me your faith apart from works, and from my works I will show you faith."

—James 2:18

Blessed are the undefiled in the way, who walk in the law of the Lord.

Blessed are they who keep His testimonies, and who seek Him with the whole heart.

They also do no iniquity; they walk in His ways.

You have commanded us to keep Your precepts diligently.

O that my ways were directed to keep Your statutes!

—**Psalm 119:1-5**

Obedience Pays Off, Cheating Plays Out

Don't be deceived: God is not mocked; for whatever a man sows, that also he will reap.

For the one who sows to the flesh will reap corruption, but the one who sows to the Spirit will reap eternal life.

So let's not get tired of well-doing, for in due season we will reap, if we don't lose heart.

—**Galatians 6:7-9**

And the angel of the Lord called unto Abraham out of heaven the second time, and said, "I have sworn by Myself," says the Lord, "for because you have done this thing and have not withheld your son—your only son—then in blessing I will bless you, and in multiplying I will multiply your seed as the stars of heaven and as the sand which is on the seashore.

"And your seed will possess the gate of his enemies, and in your seed will all the nations of the earth be blessed because you have obeyed My voice."

—**Genesis 22:15-18**

A man named Simon previously had practiced sorcery in that city and astounded the Samaritan nation, while claiming to be somebody great. . . .

When Simon saw that the Holy Spirit was given through the laying on of the apostles' hands, he offered them money, saying, "Give me this power too, so that anyone I lay hands on may receive the Holy Spirit."

But Peter told him, "May your silver be destroyed with you, because you thought the gift of God could be obtained with money!

"You have no part or share in this matter, because your heart is not right before God."

—Acts 8:9, 18-21

"No one can be a slave of two masters, since either he will hate one and love the other, or be devoted to one and despise the other. You cannot be slaves of God and of money."

—Matthew 6:24

"And you will love the Lord your God with all your heart, and with all your soul, and with all your might."

—Deuteronomy 6:5

Right Actions Come from a Clean Heart

Let the words of my mouth and the meditation of my heart be acceptable in your sight, O Lord, my strength and my redeemer.

—Psalm 19:14

How shall a young man cleanse his way? By taking heed according to Your word.

—Psalm 119:9

Finally brothers, whatever is true, whatever is honorable, whatever is righteous, whatever is pure, whatever is lovely, whatever is commendable, if there is any moral excellence and if there is anything praiseworthy, think about these things.

—Philippians 4:8

God Knows When You're Doing Your Best

But He, being full of compassion, forgave their iniquity and did not destroy them. Yes, many a time He turned His anger away and did not stir up all His wrath.

For He remembered that they were just flesh, a wind that passes away and comes not again.

—Psalm 78:38-39

The Lord is gracious and full of compassion, slow to anger and of great mercy.

The Lord is good to all, and His tender mercies are over all His works.

—Psalm 145:8-9

He will not always chide, neither will he keep His anger forever.

He has not dealt with us after our sins or rewarded us according to our iniquities.

—Psalm 103:9-10

For we have all received grace after grace from His fullness.

—John 1:16

God's Rule Is Love, His Reward Is Heaven

Since by the one man's trespass, death reigned through that one man, how much more will those who receive the overflow of grace and the gift of righteousness reign in life through the one man, Jesus Christ.

—Romans 5:17

In Him we have redemption through His blood, the forgiveness of transgressions, according to the riches of His grace that He lavished on us with all wisdom and understanding.

—Ephesians 1:7-8

For by grace you are saved through faith; and is not from yourselves, it is God's gift—not from works, so that no one can boast.

For we are His work of art, created in Christ Jesus for good works, which God prepared ahead of time that we should walk in them.

—Ephesians 2:8-10

CHECK IT OUT...

The Bible is not just a big book of rules. It's a book about winning…by the rules.

Saul—He thought he could pick and choose God's rules and get away with it. (1 Samuel 15:13-23)

Naaman—God wanted to make sure he got cured of his pride as well as his leprosy. (2 Kings 5:1-14)

Jonah—Jonah heard God's way but chose the highway. And his plans got all wet. (Jonah 1:1-17)

Rich Young Ruler—Would he be willing to obey when it cost him something? (Matthew 19:16-26)

Ananias & Sapphira—They paid a dear price for playing by their own rules. (Acts 5:1-11)

Coaching

Also, do the things which you learned and received and heard and saw in me, and the God of peace will be with you.

—PHILIPPIANS 4:9

"You'll have to switch to the pro serve grip eventually, Todd."

"But Coach, I can hit a tennis ball harder than anybody on this team."

"I know. But in a couple of years, your serves are going to come right back at you like bullets. You've got to start putting some spin on the ball—or you're gonna be eating it"

Right. What does he know? The guy can barely walk on that gimpy leg. And with those weird coke-bottle eyeglasses, he probably can't even *see* my serves.

He thinks I need *him* to tell *me* how to play? I'll show him who's boss on *this* court.

How Well Do You Take Instruction?

Holding on to discipline is a path to life, but turning your back on censure is a path to error.

—Proverbs 10:17

"Only take heed to yourself and keep your soul diligently, lest you forget the things your eyes have seen, lest they depart from your heart all the days of your life. Teach them to your sons and your sons' sons.

"Remember the day that you stood before the Lord your God in Horeb, when the Lord said to me, 'Gather the people together, and I will make them hear My words, that they may learn to fear Me all the days that they live, and that they may teach their children.' "

—Deuteronomy 4:9-10

Count on Good Role Models for Good Advice

I'm not writing these things to make you ashamed, but I'm warning you as my dear children.

For you may have myriads of instructors in Christ, but not many fathers. For in Christ Jesus I have become your father through the gospel.

Therefore I beg you, become imitators of me.

—1 Corinthians 4:14-16

But we desire each one of you to demonstrate the same earnestness to the full assurance of hope to the end, so that you may not become sluggish, but imitators of those who through faith and steadfastness are inheriting the promises.

—Hebrews 6:11-12

I thank God, whom I serve with a clear conscience from my forefathers, as without ceasing I remember you in my prayers night and day, longing to see you as I remember your tears, so that I may be filled with joy.

I call to remembrance your sincere faith which lived first in your grandmother Lois and in your mother Eunice, and I am certain also lives in you.

—2 Timothy 1:3-5

Brothers, take the prophets who spoke in the Lord's name as an example of suffering and patience.

—James 5:10

Dear friend, do not imitate what is evil, but what is good. The one who does good is of God. The one who does evil has not seen God.

—3 John 1:11

Keep Both Eyes on Jesus Christ

"Not everyone who says to Me, 'Lord, Lord!' will enter the kingdom of heaven, but the one who does the will of My Father in heaven."

—Matthew 7:21

"You call Me Teacher and Lord. This is well said, for I am."

—John 13:13

He didn't sin, neither was guile found in His mouth.

When He was reviled, He didn't answer back; when He suffered, he didn't complain, but committed Himself to Him who judges righteously.

—1 Peter 2:22-23

Accept Your Parents' Coaching, Too

Children, obey your parents in everything, for this is well pleasing in the Lord.

—Colossians 3:20

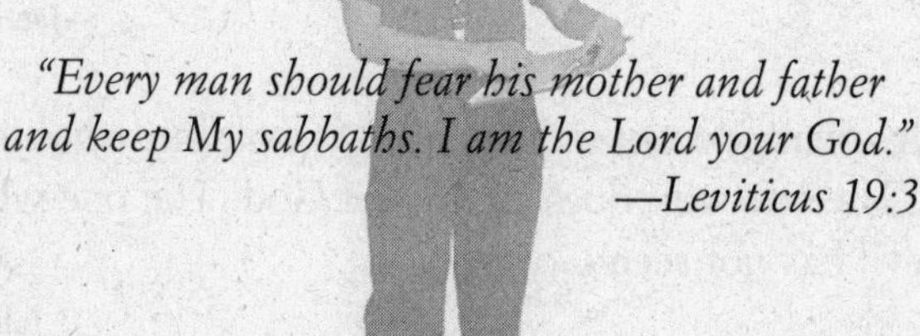

"Every man should fear his mother and father and keep My sabbaths. I am the Lord your God."

—Leviticus 19:3

My son, if you will take my words and hoard my commands for yourself, making your ear attentive to wisdom, and if you stretch your mind toward reason—indeed, if you will call out to understanding and shout out after reason, if you will seek her like money and search for her like hidden treasure, then you will understand the fear of the Lord and find the knowledge of God.

—Proverbs 2:1-5

Pay heed, my sons, to your father's discipline, and pay attention so that you may know the meaning of understanding.

For I am giving you good instruction. Do not abandon

my teaching!

When I was under the instruction of my father, tender, and my mother's one and only, he taught me and said to me, "Let your heart hold on to my words, Keep my commands and live!"

—Proverbs 4:1-4

Discipline your son and he will give you rest; he will give pleasures to your soul.

—Proverbs 29:17

Listen to your father who sired you; and do not despise your mother because she is old.

Acquire truth and do not sell wisdom and discipline and understanding.

The father of a righteous son will rejoice, and whoever sires a wise son will find joy in him.

Let your father and mother have joy; let she who bore you rejoice!

My son, give your heart to me, and keep your eyes fixed on my ways.

—Proverbs 23:22-26

You're Young—This Is Your Chance to Learn

It is good for a man to bear the yoke in his youth.

He sits alone and keeps silence because he has borne it upon him.

He puts his mouth in the dust if so be there may be hope.

He gives his cheek to him that strikes him; he is filled full with reproach.

For the Lord will not cast off for ever.

But though He causes grief, yet He will have compassion according to the multitude of his mercies.

For He does not willingly afflict nor grieve the children of men.

—Lamentations 3:27-33

Now the child Samuel ministered to the Lord before Eli. The word of the Lord was rare in those days; there was no open vision.

And during that time, when Eli was laid down in his place and his eyes had begun to get so dim that he couldn't see, when the lamp of God went out in the temple of the Lord where the ark of God was, and Samuel was laid down to sleep, the Lord called Samuel. And he answered, "Here I am."

—1 Samuel 3:1-4

You, therefore, my son, be strong in the grace which is in Christ Jesus.

And the things which you have heard from me through many witnesses, commit these to faithful men who will be capable of teaching others also.

You, share hardship with me as a good soldier of Christ Jesus.

—2 Timothy 2:1-3

Do Even More Than They Ask You To

"You have heard that it was said, 'An eye for an eye' and 'a tooth for a tooth.'

"But I tell you, don't resist an evildoer. On the contrary, if anyone slaps you on your right cheek, turn the other to him also.

"As for the one who wants to sue you and take away your shirt, let him have your coat as well.

"And if anyone forces you to go one mile, go with him two.

"Give to the one who asks you, and don't turn away from the one who wants to borrow from you."

—Matthew 5:38-41

For the grace of God that brings salvation has appeared to all men, instructing us that denying ungodliness and worldly lusts we should live soberly, righteously, and godly in the present age.

—Titus 2:12

All things are lawful for me, but all things are not helpful. All things are lawful for me, but I will not be brought under the control of any.

—1 Corinthians 6:12

All things are lawful, but not all things are helpful. All things are lawful, but not all things build up.
—1 Corinthians 10:23

So then, brothers, we are obligated, not to the flesh to live according to the flesh, because if you live according to the flesh, you are going to die; but if by the Spirit you put to death the deeds of the body, you will live.

—**Romans 8:12-13**

Then Jesus said to His disciples, "If anyone wants to come with Me, he must deny himself, take up his cross, and follow Me.

"For whoever wants to save his life will lose it, but whoever loses his life because of Me will find it.

"What will it benefit a man if he gains the whole world yet loses his life? Or what will a man give in exchange for his life?"

—**Matthew 16:24-26**

Let's See Some Hustle!

I went by the field of a lazy man and passed by the vineyard of a man without sense.

Thistles had come up everywhere, nettles covered the ground, and the stone wall was ruined.

I stared, I considered the matter, I looked, I took a lesson: "A little sleep, a little slumber, a little folding of the hands to lie down, and your poverty will come upon you like a vagrant, and your need will be like a beggar."

—**Proverbs 24:30-34**

Everyone who competes exercises self-control in all things. Now they do it to win a perishable crown, but we for an imperishable one.

I therefore run like this: not with uncertainty. This is how I fight: not as one who beats the air.

But I discipline my body and bring it into subjection,

so that, when I have preached to others, I myself won't be disqualified.

—1 Corinthians 9:25-27

For even when we were with you, we commanded you this: "If anyone doesn't want to work, neither should he eat!"

For we hear that there are some who walk among you in a disorderly way, not working at all, but they are busybodies.

Now those who are such we command and exhort by the Lord Jesus Christ that with quietness they work and eat their own bread.

—2 Thessalonians 3:10-12

Make it your ambition to lead a quiet life, to mind your own business, and to work with your own hands, as we commanded you, so that you may walk properly toward outsiders, and so you may lack nothing.

—1 Thessalonians 4:11-12

Choose Your Friends Wisely—They Coach You, Too!

Blessed is the man who doesn't walk in the counsel of the ungodly, or stands in the path of sinners, or sits in the seat of the scornful.

But his delight is in the law of the Lord, and in His law he meditates day and night.

He will be like a tree planted by rivers of water, that brings forth fruit in season. His leaf also will not wither, and whatever he does will prosper.

—Psalm 1:1-3

Do not associate with an angry man, and do not come near a furious man.

—Proverbs 22:24

A perverse man promotes conflict, and rumors separate friends.

—Proverbs 16:28

A righteous man is careful in dealing with his peers, but the way of the wicked leads them into many mistakes.

—Proverbs 12:26

Anyone who loves purity of heart has gracious lips and a king for his friend.

—Proverbs 22:11

The wounds of a friend are trustworthy; the kisses of an enemy are profuse.

—Proverbs 27:6

Oil and incense give joy to the heart. The graciousness of a friend is in his soulful counsel.

Do not abandon your friend or your father's friend, and do not go to your brother on a day of calamity. A neighbor close by is better than a brother far away.

—Proverbs 27:9-10

Good Things Happen When You Work Together

The Lord said to Moses, "Gather unto Me seventy men of the elders of Israel whom you know to be the elders of the people and officers over them, and bring them to the tabernacle of the congregation that they may stand there with you.

"And I will come down and talk with you there. I will take of the spirit which is upon you and will put it upon them, and they will bear the burden of the people with you so that you don't have to bear it by yourself alone."

—Numbers 11:16-17

Soon afterward, Jesus was traveling from one town and village to another, preaching and telling the good news of the kingdom of God.

The Twelve were with Him, and also some women who had been healed of evil spirits and sicknesses: Mary, called Magdalene, from whom seven demons had come out; Joanna the wife of Chuza, Herod's steward; Susanna; and many others who were supporting them from their possessions.

—Luke 8:1-3

After this the Lord appointed seventy others, and He sent them ahead of Him in pairs to every town and place where He Himself was about to go.

He told them: "The harvest is abundant, but the workers are few. Therefore, pray to the Lord of the harvest to send out workers into His harvest."

—Luke 10:1-2

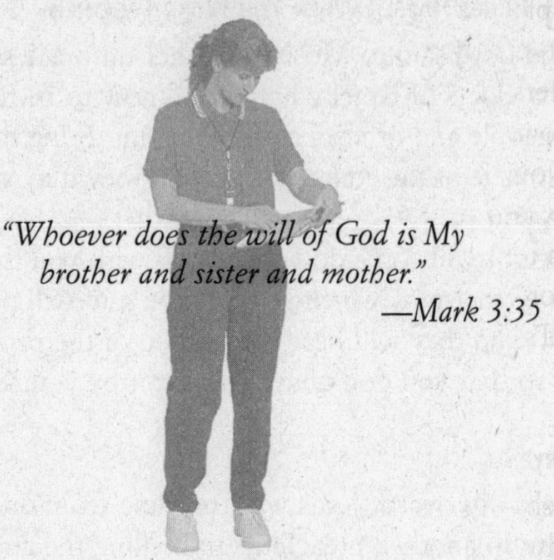

"Whoever does the will of God is My brother and sister and mother."
—*Mark 3:35*

Christian Living Is a Team Sport

Better are two than one because there is a good reward for them in their toil.

For if either of them falls, his companion can lift him up, but pity the one who falls and there is no one to lift him up.

Furthermore, if two lie down together, then they can keep warm, but how can one person keep warm?

And if one is overpowered, then two can stand against him. Indeed, the three-fold cord is not easily broken.

—Ecclesiastes 4:9-12

So when they recognized the grace given to me, James, Cephas, and John—who seemed to be pillars—gave Barnabas and me the right hand of fellowship, in order that we indeed should go to the Gentiles, as they also to the circumcised.

—Galatians 2:9

I planted, Apollos watered, but God gave the growth.
So then neither is the one who plants or the one who waters important, but the growth-giving God is the one who matters!
Now the one who plants and the one who waters are one, and each will receive an individual reward in proportion to his labor.
For we are God's co-workers. You are God's field, God's building.

—1 Corinthians 3:6-9

Everybody Stick Together

Behold, how good and how pleasant it is for brothers to dwell together in unity!

—Psalm 133:1

And when he had made an end of speaking to Saul, the soul of Jonathan was knit with the soul of David, and Jonathan loved him as his own soul.
And Saul took David that day and would not let him go home to his father's house anymore.
Then Jonathan and David made a covenant, because he loved him as his own soul.
And Jonathan stripped himself of the robe that was on him and gave it to David, along with his garments—even down to his sword, his bow, and his girdle.

—1 Samuel 18:1-4

I want their hearts to be encouraged and knit together in love, so that they may have all the riches of assured understanding and have the knowledge of God's mystery—Christ.

—Colossians 2:2

Now we ask you, brothers, to recognize those who labor among you, who lead you in the Lord and admonish you.

Esteem them very highly in love because of their work. Be at peace among yourselves.

—1 Thessalonians 5:12-13

So then, my beloved brothers and my joy and crown, in this way stand firm in the Lord, dear friends.

I encourage Euodia and I encourage Synteche to agree in the Lord.

Yes, I also sincerely ask you, true companion, help these women who have struggled together with me for the gospel, with Clement also, and the rest of the co-workers whose names are in the book of life.

—Philippians 4:1-3

Christ Himself gave apostles, prophets, evangelists, pastors and teachers, to train the saints for the work of ministry, to build up the body of the Messiah, until we all arrive at the unity of the faith and the knowledge of the Son of God to a complete man, to the measure of the maturity of the Messiah's fullness.

—Ephesians 4:11-13

But I beg you, brothers, in the name of our Lord Jesus Christ, that you all say the same thing, and that there be no divisions among you, but that you be perfectly united in the same mind and in the same opinion.

—1 Corinthians 1:10

WE'RE ALL IN THIS THING TOGETHER

When the scribes of the Pharisees saw that He was eating with sinners and tax collectors, they asked His disciples, "Why does He eat with tax collectors and sinners?"

When Jesus heard this, He told them, "Those who are well don't need a doctor, but the sick do need one. I didn't come to call the righteous, but sinners."

—Mark 2:16-17

"I have spread out My hands all day to a rebellious people who walk in a way that is not good, who walk after their own thoughts—a people who provoke me to anger continually to my face, who sacrifice in gardens and burn incense upon altars of brick, who remain among the graves and lodge in the monuments, who eat pig's flesh and the broth of abominable things in their vessels, who say, 'Stand by yourself; don't come near to me, for I am holier than you.' "

"These are a smoke in My nose, a fire that burns all the day."

—Isaiah 65:2-5

They killed both the Lord Jesus and the prophets and have persecuted us.

Also they do not please God and are contrary to all people, forbidding us to speak to the Gentiles that they may be saved, so as always to fill up the measure of their sins. But wrath has come on them to the uttermost.

—1 Thessalonians 2:15-16

For you are all sons of God through faith in Christ Jesus, because as many of you as have been baptized into Christ have put on Christ.

There is neither Jew nor Greek, neither slave nor free, neither male nor female; for you are all one in Christ Jesus.

But if you are Christ's, then you are Abraham's seed, heirs according to the promise.

—Galatians 3:26-29

Check It Out...

You'll never have what it takes until you can take a little coaching. See for yourself.

Hophni & Phinehas—They'd have done a lot better if they'd listened to their dad. (1 Samuel 2:12-25)

James & John—They asked the wrong question but at least to the right Person. (Mark 9:35-45)

Prodigal Son—He went into the real world without a really good game plan. (Luke 15:11-24)

Apollos—He could wow people with his words, but he wanted his words to be right. (Acts 18:24-28)

Timothy—Paul had been like a father to him, and Timothy wanted to please him. (2 Timothy 2:15-26)

Defeat

O God, I trust in You. Don't let me be ashamed. Don't let my enemies triumph over me.

—Psalm 25:2

I had him on points. I even had him half-way pinned—twice!

Then a crummy little take-down. A twist of the hips. Before I know it, he's digging his chin into my chest and, like, there's no way I'm getting up.

See, you can be stronger.
You can be quicker.
You can have more guts.

But you've gotta be smarter, too. I mean, I made a wrong move, and the guy just took over from there.

I've gotta be better than that. I've gotta want it more.

No way he's ever doing that to me again. No way!

Ringside at an Early Wrestling Match

Jacob was left alone, and there he wrestled with a man until the breaking of the day.

When the man saw that he could not prevail against Jacob, he touched the hollow of his thigh, and the hollow of Jacob's thigh fell out of joint as he wrestled with him.

Then the man said, "Let me go, for day is breaking." And Jacob said, "I will not let you go unless you bless me."

—Genesis 32:24-26

He said to him, "What is your name?" And he said, "Jacob."

He said, "Your name will not be called Jacob anymore, but Israel, for you have struggled with God and with men and have prevailed."

And Jacob asked him, "Tell me your name, I pray you." And he said, "Why do you ask My name?" And He blessed him there.

And Jacob called the name of the place Peniel—"for I have seen God face to face and my life is preserved."

—Genesis 32:27-30

And as he passed over Penuel, the sun rose upon him and he limped because of his thigh.

That is why the children of Israel do not eat of the muscle that shrank (which is in the hollow of the thigh) even to this day, because he touched the hollow of Jacob's thigh in the muscle that shrank.

—Genesis 32:31-32

There's Nothing New About Losing

" 'They are destroyed from morning to evening. They perish forever without any regarding it.' "

—Job 4:20

Now the Philistines fought against Israel, and the men of Israel fled from before the Philistines and fell down dead in mount Gilboa.

And the Philistines followed hard upon Saul and his sons, and they killed Jonathan, Abinadab, and Malchishua, Saul's sons. . . .

So Saul and his three sons died, as well as his armor-bearer and all his men that same day together.

—1 Samuel 31:1-2, 6

"Saul and Jonathan were lovely and pleasant in their lives, and in their death they were not divided. They were swifter than eagles; they were stronger than lions.

"You daughters of Israel, weep over Saul, who clothed you in scarlet and with other delights, who put ornaments of gold upon your apparel.

"How are the mighty fallen in the midst of the battle! O Jonathan, you were killed in your high places."

—2 Samuel 1:23-25

In the ninth year and the tenth month of Zedekiah king of Judah, Nebuchadnezzar, king of Babylon, and all his army came against Jerusalem and besieged it. . . .

And when Zedekiah the king of Judah saw them and all the men of war, they fled and went forth out of the city by night by the way of the king's garden, by the gate between the two walls. And he went out the way of the plain.

But the Chaldeans' army pursued after them and overtook Zedekiah in the plains of Jericho. And when they had taken him, they brought him up to Nebuchadnezzar, king of Babylon, to Riblah in the land of Hamath, where he gave judgment upon him.

Then the king of Babylon killed the sons of Zedekiah in Riblah before his eyes. He also killed all the nobles of Judah.

What's more, he put out Zedekiah's eyes and bound him with chains to carry him to Babylon.

—Jeremiah 39:1, 4-7

Losing Hurts, But God Comforts

"And when they ask you, 'Why are you sighing?' you should answer, "Because of the tidings, because it comes. And every heart will melt, and all hands will be feeble, and every spirit will faint, and all knees will be weak as water.' "

—Ezekiel 21:7a

When I would comfort myself against sorrow, my heart is faint in me.

—Jeremiah 8:18

My eyes fill with tears, my bowels are troubled, my liver is poured upon the earth, for the destruction of the daughter of my people, because the children and the babies swoon in the streets of the city.

They say to their mothers, "Where is corn and wine?" when they swoon as the wounded in the streets of the city, when their soul is poured out into their mothers' bosom. . . .

Arise, cry out in the night. In the beginning of the watches, pour out your heart like water before the face of the Lord. Lift up your hands toward Him for the life of your young children that faint for hunger in the top of every street.

—Lamentations 2:11-12, 19

But now, the Lord that created you, O Jacob—He that formed you, O Israel—says, "Do not be afraid, for I have redeemed you. I have called you by your name; you are Mine.

"When you pass through the waters, I will be with you. When you pass through the rivers, they will not overflow you. When you walk through the fire, you will not be burned, neither will the flame kindle upon you.

"For I am the Lord your God, the Holy One of Israel, your Savior."

—Isaiah 43:1-3a

Defeat Builds Character

We are pressured in every way, but are not crushed; we are perplexed but not in despair; we are persecuted but not abandoned; we are struck down, but not destroyed.

We are always bearing the death of Jesus in our body, so that the life of Jesus may be exhibited in our body.

—2 Corinthians 4:8-10

"But I have prayed for you, that your faith may not fail. And you, when you have turned back, strengthen your brothers."

—Luke 22:32

Though the fig tree does not bud and there is no grape on the vines, though the crop of olive fields produce no food, though He cuts us off from the sheep pen and there are no cattle in the stalls—yet I will rejoice in the Lord! I will celebrate the God of my salvation!

O Lord Yahweh, my strength! He makes my feet like those of a deer, and He lifts me to the heights!

—**Habakkuk 3:17-19**

"Come to Me, all you who are weary and burdened, and I will give you rest.

"Take My yoke upon you and learn from Me, because I am gentle and humble in heart, and you will find rest for your souls.

"For My yoke is easy and My burden is light."

—**Matthew 11:28-30**

GOD STILL THINKS YOU'RE SOMETHING

I remembered God and was troubled. I complained and my spirit was overwhelmed.

You hold my eyes awake. I am so troubled that I cannot speak.

I have considered the days of old, the years of ancient times.

I call to remembrance my song in the night. I commune with my own heart and my spirit makes diligent search.

Will the Lord cast off forever, and will He be favorable to us no more?

Is his mercy clean gone forever? Does His promise fail for evermore?

Has God forgotten to be gracious? Has He in anger shut up His tender mercies?

—**Psalm 77:3-9**

Why do you say, O Jacob, and speak, O Israel, "My way is hidden from the Lord and my judgment is passed over from my God?"

Have you not known? Have you not heard that the everlasting God, the Lord, the Creator of the ends of the earth, does not faint or become weary? There is no searching of His understanding.

—Isaiah 40:27-28

"If you, then, who are evil, know how to give good gifts to your children, how much more will your Father in heaven give good things to those who ask Him!"

—Matthew 7:11

"Can a mother forget her nursing child? Can she not have compassion on the son of her womb? Yes, they may forget, yet I will not forget you.

—Isaiah 49:15

Live to Play Another Day

O Lord, open my lips, and my mouth will show forth Your praise.

For You do not desire sacrifice or I would give it. You do not take delight in burnt offerings.

The sacrifices of God are a broken spirit. A broken and a contrite heart, O God, You will not despise.

—Psalm 51:15-17

"Because I will be merciful to their unrighteousnesses, and their sins I will by no means remember anymore."

—Hebrews 8:12

Therefore, brothers, since we have boldness to enter the sanctuary by the blood of Jesus by the new and living way which He has opened for us—through the veil (that is, His flesh)—and since we have a great High Priest over the house of God, let us approach with a true heart in full assurance of faith, our hearts having been sprinkled from an evil conscience and our bodies having been bathed in pure water.

—Hebrews 10:19-22

By this means love has been brought to maturity with us, so that we may have confidence in the day of judgment, because just as He is, so we are in this world.

—1 John 4:17

Trust God for the Victory

"After these events, I will pour out My Spirit on all humanity. Then your sons and your daughters will prophecy, your old men will dream dreams, your young men will see visions.

"Then, in those days, I will also pour out My Spirit on My servants, both men and women.

"Then I will set wonders in the heavens and the earth—blood and fire and columns of smoke.

"The sun will be turned to darkness and the moon to

blood, before the coming of the great and fearful Day of the Lord.

"And so it will be that everyone who calls on the name of the Lord will be delivered, because on Mount Zion and in Jerusalem there will be those who experience deliverance, just as the Lord said, even among the survivors whom the Lord calls."

—Joel 2:28-32

"I also will ask the Father, and He will give you another Counselor to be with you forever.

"He is the Spirit of truth, whom the world is unable to receive because it doesn't see Him or know Him. But you do know Him, because He remains with you and will be in you."

—John 14:16-17

"Peace I leave with you. My peace I give to you. I do not give to you as the world gives. Your heart must not be troubled or fearful."

—John 14:27

Watch Your Mouth!

Now especially, my brothers, do not swear, either by heaven or by earth or by any other oath. But let your "Yes" be "Yes" and your "No" be "No," so that you won't fall under judgment.

—James 5:12

" 'Whom have you reproached and blasphemed? And against whom have you exalted your voice and lifted up your eyes on high? It has been against the Holy One of Israel.' "

—2 Kings 19:22

Remember this: the enemy has reproached, O Lord, and the foolish people have blasphemed Your name.

—Psalm 74:18

As he loved cursing, so let it come unto him; as he delighted not in blessing, so let it be far from him.

—Psalm 109:17

If anyone thinks he is religious but does not bridle his tongue, he deceives his own heart. The religion of such a person is useless.

—James 1:26

The tongue is a fire. The tongue is made a world of wickedness among our members. It pollutes the whole body, sets the course of life on fire, and is set on fire by hell.

—James 3:6

With it we bless our Lord and Father, and with it we curse men who are made in God's image.

A blessing and a curse come out of the same mouth! My brothers, these things ought not to be so.

—James 3:9-10

For in many respects we all stumble. If anyone does not slip up in word, he is a perfect man who is able also to hold the whole body in check.

—James 3:2

Keep Getting Defeated by Temptation?

Consider it all joy, my brothers, whenever you undergo a variety of trials, since you know that the approved quality of your faith produces endurance.

—James 1:2-3

Blessed is the man who endures trial, because when he becomes approved he will receive the crown of life which God has promised to those who love Him.

—James 1:12

No temptation has overtaken you except such as is common to humanity. But God is faithful, who will not allow you to be tempted beyond what you are able. But with the temptation He will also make the way of escape, so you may be able to bear it.

—1 Corinthians 10:13

Since, then, the children participate in blood and flesh, Christ Himself likewise partook with them, in order that through death He might destroy the one who has the power over death—that is, the devil—and release all those who through fear of death were subject to slavery all their lives. . . .

Hence, He had to be made like His brothers in everything, in order that He might become a compassionate and faithful High Priest in the things pertaining to God, to atone for the sins of the people.

For since He Himself has suffered, having been tempted, He is able to come to the aid of those who are tempted.

—Hebrews 2:14, 16-18

God Can Help You Tackle the Toughest Sin

Then I heard a loud voice in heaven say: "The salvation and the power and the kingdom of our God and the authority of His Messiah have now come, because the accuser of our brothers has been thrown out—the one who accuses them before our God day and night."

—Revelation 12:10

Unless the Lord had been my help, my soul would have almost dwelt in silence. When I said, "My foot is slipping," Your mercy, O Lord, held me up.

—Psalm 94:17-18

"Therefore be alert, since you don't know what day your Lord is coming.

"But know this: If the homeowner had known what time the thief was coming, he would have stayed alert and not let his house be broken into.

"This is why you also should get ready, because the Son of Man is coming at an hour you do not expect."

—Matthew 24:42-44

Christians Already Know They Win in the End

"The Lord rewarded me according to my righteousness; according to the cleanness of my hands He has repaid me.

"For I have kept the ways of the Lord and have not wickedly departed from my God.

"For all His judgments were before me. And as for His statutes, I did not depart from them.

"I was also upright before Him and have kept myself from iniquity.

"Therefore the Lord has repaid me according to my righteousness, according to my cleanness in His eyesight."

—2 Samuel 22:21-25

Now may the God of peace Himself sanctify you completely. And may your whole spirit, soul, and body be kept blameless at the coming of our Lord Jesus Christ.

He who calls you is faithful, who also will do it.

—1 Thessalonians 5:23-24

Blessed be the Lord, for He has showed me His marvelous kindness in a strong city.

For I said in my haste, "I am cut off from before Your eyes." Nevertheless, You heard the voice of my prayer when I cried out to You.

O love the Lord, all you His saints, for the Lord preserves the faithful and plentifully rewards the proud man.

Be of good courage and He will strengthen your heart, all you that hope in the Lord.

—Psalm 31:21-24

Therefore, no condemnation now exists for those in Christ Jesus.

For the Spirit's law of life in Christ Jesus has set you free from the law of sin and of death.

For what the law was unable to do because it was limited by the flesh, God did by sending His own Son in flesh like ours under sin's domain, and as a sin offering He condemned sin in His flesh.

He did this so that the law's requirement would be accomplished in us who do not walk according to the flesh but according to the Spirit.

—Romans 8:1-4

"Let the unrighteous go on in unrighteousness; let the filthy go on being made filthy; let the righteous go on in righteousness; and let the holy go on being made holy."

—Revelation 22:11

CHECK IT OUT . . .

God's people have been facing defeat for a long time—and living to play another day.

Adam & Eve—Yes, they lost in a big way, but God put their enemy in his place. (Genesis 3:1-15)

David—Caught redhanded, he admitted his mistake and asked for forgiveness. (2 Samuel 12:1-13)

Jeremiah—Life beat him up, but he knew God would have the last word. (Lamentations 3:10-26)

Adulterous Woman—This could have been the end for her... or a whole new beginning. (John 8:1-11)

John Mark—He fell out of favor with Paul...for a little while. (Acts 15:36-40; see 2 Timothy 4:11, too)

Perseverance

Don't you know that those who run in a stadium all run, but only one receives the prize? Run in such a way that you may win.

—1 Corinthians 9:24

You get so tired, you stop caring about the plays.

YOU GUYS GOTTA GET BACK ON DEFENSE—QUICK!

I know, but you get so tired.

OK, IT'S TIME TO GO WITH THE FULL-COURT PRESS. RUN 'EM INTO THE GROUND, GUYS! GO AFTER THE BALL! SUCK IT UP! LET'S GO!

You get so tired, you just want the clock to speed up.

HEY, WAKE UP! DO YOU GUYS SEE THE SCORE?
WE'RE GIVING THIS THING AWAY!

Right now, I'm just watching the clock.

HUSTLE! HUSTLE!

You get so tired.

Everybody Gets Tired

He gives power to the faint; and to those who have no might, He increases their strength.

Even the youths can become faint and weary, and the young men can utterly fall.

But they that wait upon the Lord will renew their strength. They will mount up with wings as eagles. They will run and not be weary; they will walk and not faint.

—Isaiah 40:29-31

Therefore we do not lose heart, but even if our outer self is being ruined, our inner self is being renewed day after day.

—2 Corinthians 4:16

My days are like a shadow that declines, and I am withered like grass.

But You, O Lord, will endure forever, and Your remembrance to all generations.

—Psalm 102:11-12

So strengthen the weakened hands and the paralyzed knees, and make straight paths for your feet, so that the lame may not be dislocated, but rather may be healed.

—Hebrews 12:12-13

Nobody Said It Would Be Easy

No one should be shaken by their afflictions. For you yourselves know that we are appointed to this.

—1 Thessalonians 3:3

For we know that the whole creation has been groaning together with labor pains up until now.

And not only that, but we ourselves also who have the Spirit as the firstfruits—we also groan within ourselves, eagerly waiting for adoption, the redemption of our bodies.

—Romans 8:22-23

Three times I was beaten with rods. Once I was stoned. Three times I was shipwrecked. A night and a day I have spent in the ocean.

I have been on journeys frequently, facing dangers from rivers, dangers from robbers, dangers from my own people, dangers from the Gentiles, dangers in the city, dangers in the wilderness, dangers on the sea, dangers among false brothers.

I have known labor and toil, sleepless nights very often, hunger and thirst, going without food very often, cold and lack of clothing.

—2 Corinthians 11:25-27

What a wretched man I am! Who will rescue me from this body of death?

—Romans 7:24

But thanks be to God, who always leads us in a triumphal procession in Christ, and through us spreads the fragrance of the knowledge of Him in every place.

—2 Corinthians 2:14

God Is There in the Tough Times

He will deliver you in six troubles. Yes, even in seven, no evil will touch you.

—Job 5:19

Blessed be the God and Father of our Lord Jesus Christ, the Father of mercies and the God of all comfort, who comforts us in all our trouble, so that we may be able to comfort those who are in any trouble, through the comfort with which we ourselves are comforted by God.

—2 Corinthians 1:3-4

Though I walk in the midst of trouble, You will revive me. You will stretch out Your hand against the wrath of my enemies, and Your right hand will save me.

—Psalm 138:7

The Lord is good, a stronghold in a day of distress, knowing those who take refuge in Him.

—Nahum 1:7

Dig In—You Can Make It

I will go into Your house with burnt offerings. I will pay You my vows, which my lips have uttered and my mouth has spoken when I was in trouble.

—Psalm 66:13-14

" 'Behold, the days come,' says the Lord, 'that I will perform that good thing which I have promised to the house of Israel and to the house of Judah.' "

—Jeremiah 33:14

"And I will strengthen them in the Lord, and they will walk up and down in His name," says the Lord.

—Zechariah 10:12

For as many promises of God as there are, in Him they are Yes. Therefore also through him is the Amen, for the glory of God through us.

Now God is the one who confirms us with you for Christ, and has anointed us.

—2 Corinthians 1:20-21

Stick with It, No Matter How Hard It Gets

Anyone who loves a good time will become needy. No one who loves wine and oil will get rich.

—Proverbs 21:17

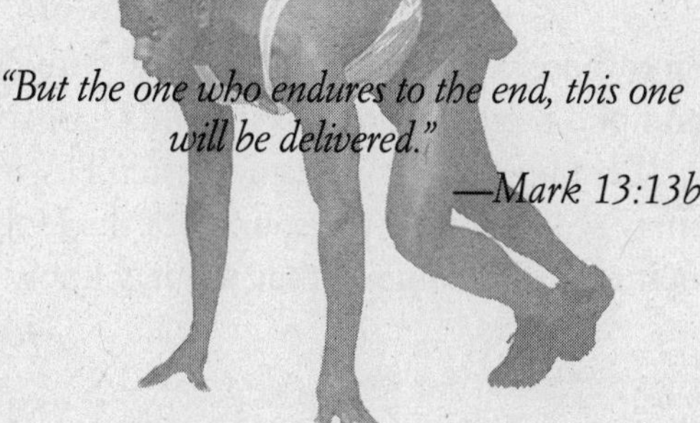

"But the one who endures to the end, this one will be delivered."

—Mark 13:13b

See, we regard those who have endured as blessed. You have heard of the endurance of Job and have seen the conclusion brought by the Lord since the Lord is extremely sympathetic and compassionate.

—James 5:11

For this reason I also suffer these things, but I am not ashamed, because I know in whom I have believed, and I am persuaded that he is able to guard what I have entrusted to him until that Day.

—2 Timothy 1:12

"In the same way, therefore, every one of you who does not say goodbye to all his possessions cannot be My disciple."

—Luke 14:33

God Makes You Strong in the Struggle

"Woe to him that strives with his Maker! Let the pots strive with the other pots of the earth. Should the clay say to him who fashions it, 'What are You making?' or your work say, 'He has no hands'?"

—Isaiah 45:9

Woe unto those who draw their iniquity with cords of vanity, and pull their sin along as if with a cart rope—who say, "Let Him make speed and hasten His work so that we may see it, and let the counsel of the Holy One of Israel draw near and come so that we may know it!"

—Isaiah 5:18-19

Then Job answered the Lord, "I know that You can do everything and that no thought can be withheld from You. . . .

"I have heard of You by the hearing of the ear, but now my eyes have seen You."

—Job 42:1-2, 5

"Does he thank that slave because he did what was commanded?

"In the same way, when you have done all that you were commanded, you should say, 'We are good-for-nothing slaves. We've only done our duty.' "

—Luke 17:9-10

For consider Him who has endured such opposition by sinners against Himself, lest you grow weary and faint in your souls.

—Hebrews 12:3

Finish Strong—You Can Rest Later

And others experienced mockings and scourgings, and in addition, bonds and imprisonment.

They were stoned, they were sawn in two, they were murdered by the sword, they wandered about in sheepskins and goatskins, while being destitute, afflicted, maltreated, of whom the world was not worthy, wandering in deserts and mountains and caves and in the holes of the ground.

—Hebrews 11:36-38

And not only that, but we also rejoice in our afflictions, because we know that affliction produces endurance, endurance produces proven character, and proven character produces hope.

—Romans 5:3-4

We ourselves brag about you among the congregations of God for your patience and faith in all your persecutions and tribulations that you endure, which is clear evidence of God's righteous judgment, that you may be counted worthy of God's kingdom for which you also suffer.

—2 Thessalonians 1:4-5

By faith Moses left Egypt, though not because of the king's anger, for he persevered because he was seeing the invisible God.

—Hebrews 11:27

"Don't work for the food that perishes but for the food that lasts for eternal life, which the Son of Man will give you, because on Him God the Father has set His seal of approval."

—John 6:27

Then I heard a voice from heaven saying, "Write: Blessed are the dead who die in the Lord from now on."

"Yes," says the Spirit, "let them rest from their labors, for their works follow them!"

—Revelation 14:13

Consequently, there remains a Sabbath rest for God's people.

—Hebrews 4:9

God Will Always Be Enough

And my God will supply all your needs according to His riches in glory in Christ Jesus.

—**Philippians 4:19**

"There is salvation in no one else, for there is no other name under heaven given to people by which we must be saved."

—**Acts 4:12**

"But He saves the poor from the sword, from their mouth, and from the hand of the mighty.

"So the poor have hope, and iniquity stops her mouth."

—**Job 5:15-16**

"When the poor and needy seek water and there is none, and when their tongue fails for thirst, I the Lord will hear them. I the God of Israel will not forsake them."

—**Isaiah 41:17**

For the Lord is good; His mercy is everlasting; and His truth endures to all generations.

—**Psalm 100:5**

Therefore, we may say with confidence, "The Lord is my helper and I will not fear. What can man do to me?"

—**Hebrews 13:6**

He Has Endured a Lot for You

Surely He has borne our griefs and carried our sorrows, yet we thought of Him as stricken, smitten of God and afflicted.

But He was wounded for our transgressions. He was

bruised for our iniquities. The chastisement of our peace was upon Him, and with His stripes we are healed.

—Isaiah 53:4-5

For Christ also has suffered once for sins—the just for the unjust—that he might bring us to God, being put to death in the flesh, but brought to life by the Spirit.

—1 Peter 3:18

For rarely will someone die for a just person—though for a good person perhaps someone might even dare to die.
But God proves His own love for us in that while we were still sinners, Christ died for us!

—Romans 5:7-8

Are You Getting Your Second Wind?

"For I assure you: If you have faith the size of a mustard seed, you will tell this mountain, 'Move from here to there,' and it will move. Nothing will be impossible for you."

—Matthew 17:20b

"If you remain in Me and My words remain in you, ask whatever you want and it will be done for you.
"My Father is glorified by this: that you produce much fruit and prove to be My disciples."

—John 15:7-8

Give us help from trouble, for the help of man is vain.
Through God we will do valiantly, for it is He that will tread down our enemies.

—Psalm 60:11-12

And who is it that is a victor over the world?
It is none other than the one who believes
that Jesus is the Son of God!

—1 John 5:5

PRAY THROUGH THE PAIN

Very early in the morning, while it was still dark, Jesus got up, went out, and made His way to a deserted place. And He was praying there.

—Mark 1:35

Jesus spoke these things, then raised His eyes to heaven, and said: "Father, the hour has come. Glorify Your Son so that the Son may glorify You."

—John 17:1

Now in this hope we were saved, yet hope that is seen is not hope, because who hopes for what he sees?

And if we hope for what we do not see, we eagerly wait for it with patience.

In the same way the Spirit also joins to help in our weakness, because we do not know how we ought to pray, but the Spirit Himself intercedes for us with unspoken groanings.

And He who searches the heart knows the Spirit's way of thinking, because He intercedes for the saints according to the will of God.

—Romans 8:24-27

Is anyone among you suffering? Let him pray. Is anyone cheerful? Let him sing.

Is anyone among you sick? Let him call for the elders of the congregation, and let them pray over him after anointing him with olive oil in the name of the Lord.

The prayer of faith will save the sick person, and the Lord will raise him up. And if he has committed sins, they will be forgiven him.

—James 5:13-15

And we receive from Him whatever we ask, because we keep His commands and do what is pleasing in His sight.

—1 John 3:22

Therefore, confess your sins to one another and pray for one another that you may be healed. The energizing prayer of a righteous man accomplishes much.

Elijah was a man with feelings like our own, and he prayed earnestly for it not to rain, and it did not rain on the earth for three years and six months.

And he prayed again, and heaven gave rain and the earth produced its fruit.

—James 5:16-18

Pray without ceasing.

—1 Thessalonians 5:17

All That Hard Work Will Pay Off

But the path of the righteous is like the breaking of morning light, shining brighter and brighter until the sure light of day.

—Proverbs 4:18

So then, my beloved, just as you have always obeyed, not only in my presence, but now much more in my absence, work out your own salvation with fear and trembling.

For it is God who is working in you both to will and to work for His pleasure.

—Philippians 2:12-13

Slaves, obey your earthly masters in everything, not only while being watched and in order to please them, but wholeheartedly, fearing the Lord.

Whatever you may do, do it from the heart, as for the Lord and not for men, knowing that from the Lord you will receive the inheritance as your reward, for you are slaves of the Lord Christ.

—Colossians 3:22-24

Do all things without grumbling and arguing, in order that you may become blameless and pure children of God, without blemish in the midst of a crooked and depraved generation, among whom you shine forth as lights in the world.

—Philippians 2:14-15

"But seek first the kingdom of God and His righteousness, and all these things will be provided for you.

"Therefore don't worry about tomorrow, because tomorrow will worry about itself. Each day has enough trouble of its own."

—Matthew 6:33-34

Never Give Up

As you therefore have received Christ Jesus the Lord, keep walking in Him, rooted and built up in Him and established in the faith, just as you were taught, abounding in thanksgiving.

—Colossians 2:6-7

This is the confidence which we have towards Him, that if we ask anything according to His will He listens to us. And if we know that He listens to us in whatever we may ask, we know that we have the requests which we have made of Him.

—1 John 5:14-15

Now to Him who is able to do above and beyond all that we ask or think according to the power that works in you—to Him be glory in the church and in Christ Jesus to all generations forever and ever. Amen.

—Ephesians 3:20-21

CHECK IT OUT . . .

The Bible reminds us that even when we think we can't go on, we can—with God's help.

Jacob—Tricked out of his reward for seven years' work, he worked seven more. (Genesis 29:15-30)

Joseph—Already in jail for something he didn't do, he had to stay even longer. (Genesis 40:1-23)

Nehemiah—The walls of Jerusalem would be rebuilt if it was the last thing he did. (Nehemiah 4:7-23)

John the Baptist—He was in prison for doing right, but happy with God's approval. (Matthew 11:1-11)

Jesus—He could have put a stop to His own suffering, but He wasn't backing down. (Luke 22:39-46)

Discipline

No one serving as a soldier gets entangled in everyday affairs, so that he may please the one who enlisted him as a soldier.

—2 Timothy 2:4

Yeah, I know you can dog it if you want. Lots of kids just want that letter on their jacket at the end of the season. But if you're going to be good—I mean, really good—you have to work at it.

I want to be in that crowd.

If you're going to excel, you're in the weight room, you're doing leapfrogs around the house after supper. Maybe you run with ankle weights, or squeeze a rubber ball all day, just to strengthen your grip. You eat right and hit the curfews. You sure don't smoke or drink or eat a lot of junk.

You see, it all adds up. It gives you an edge. A lot of kids are born with talent, but they waste every bit of it.

It takes work—hard work—to be a real winner.

It Takes Discipline to Be a Winner

Teach me, O Lord, the way of Your statutes, and I will keep them to the end.

—Psalm 119:33

With my whole heart I have sought You. O do not let wander from Your commandments.

—Psalm 119:10

Cause me to hear Your lovingkindness in the morning, for I trust in You. Cause me to know the way in which I should walk, for I lift up my soul to You.

—Psalm 143:8

"But if a man is righteous and does that which is lawful and right. . .and has not oppressed anyone, but has restored to the debtor his pledge; has spoiled no one by violence; has given his bread to the hungry and has covered the naked with a garment; has not given forth his money on interest or has taken any increase; has withdrawn his hand from iniquity and has executed true judgment between man and man; has walked in My statutes and has kept My judgments to deal truly, he is righteous. He will surely live," says the Lord God.

—Ezekiel 18:5, 7-9

It's a Straight Walk Down a Sure Path

"And now, Israel, what does the Lord your God require of you, but to fear the Lord your God, to walk in all His ways, to love Him and to serve the Lord your God with all your heart and with all your soul, to keep the commandments and statutes of the Lord, which I command you this day for your good?"

—Deuteronomy 10:12-13

Your eyes should look straight ahead. Keep even your eyelids directly in front of you!

—Proverbs 4:25

Do not veer to the right or to the left. Keep your feet from evil.

—Proverbs 4:27

For the ways of a man lie directly in front of the Lord's eyes, and He observes all his tracks.

—Proverbs 5:21

"As for God, His way is perfect. The word of the Lord is tried. He is a buckler to all those who trust in Him.

"For who is God except the Lord? And who is a rock except our God?

"God is my strength and power, and He makes my way perfect.

"He makes my feet like hinds' feet and sets me upon my high places."

—2 Samuel 22:31-34

Hard Work Will Get You Noticed

"You are the light of the world. A city situated on a hill cannot be hidden.

"No one lights a lamp and puts it under a basket, but rather on a lampstand, and it gives light for all who are in the house.

"In the same way, let your light shine before men, so that they may see your good works and give glory to your Father in heaven."

—Matthew 5:14-16

The night is nearly over and the daylight is near, so let us discard the deeds of darkness and put on the armor of light.

Let us walk with decency, as in the daylight—not in carousing and drunkenness, not in sexual impurity and promiscuity, not in quarreling and jealousy.

But put on the Lord Jesus Christ, and make no plans to satisfy the fleshly desires.

—Romans 13:12-14

I, therefore, the prisoner in the Lord, exhort you to walk worthy of the calling to which you were called, with all humility and gentleness, with patience tolerating one another in love.

—Ephesians 4:1-2

For this reason, from the day we heard it, we have not ceased praying for you and asking that you may be filled with the knowledge of His will in all spiritual wisdom and understanding, so that you may walk worthy of the Lord, fully pleasing to Him, as you bear fruit in every good work and as you grow in the knowledge of God.

May you be made strong with all the strength that comes from His glorious power, and may you be prepared to endure everything with patience, with joy, giving thanks to the Father, who has enabled you to share in the inheritance of the saints in the light.

—Colossians 1:9-12

Keep your conversation honest among the Gentiles, so that even when they speak against you as evildoers, they may—by your good works, which they will behold—glorify God in the day of visitation.

—1 Peter 2:12

Since all these things are to be destroyed in this way, what sort of persons should you be in holy conduct and godliness, as you look forward to and earnestly desire the day of God, because of which the heavens, being set on fire, will be destroyed, and the elements will melt with intense heat?

But, in accordance with His promise, we wait for new heavens and a new earth, in which righteousness is at home.

Therefore, dear friends, as you're waiting for these things, strive to be found by Him in peace, spotless and blameless.

—2 Peter 3:11-14

But grow in the grace and knowledge of our Lord and Savior Jesus Christ. To Him be the glory both now and to the day of eternity! Amen.

—2 Peter 3:18

Work Hard to Stay in Shape

Dear friend, I pray that you may do well in every way and be in physical health, as your soul is well!

—3 John 1:2

When you walk, your step will not be impeded. Even if you run, you will not be tripped up.

—Proverbs 4:12

Or don't you know that your body is a sanctuary of the Holy Spirit who is in you, whom you have from God, and you don't belong to yourself?

For you were bought at a price; therefore glorify God in your body.

—1 Corinthians 6:19-20

Therefore, brothers, by the mercies of God, I urge you to present your bodies as a living sacrifice, holy and pleasing to God. This is your spiritual worship.

—Romans 12:1

For our citizenship resides in heaven, from where also we eagerly wait for the Savior, the Lord Jesus Christ, who will change the form of our lowly body to the same form as His body of glory, according to the inner working of His power and subjection of all things to Himself.

—Philippians 3:20-21

Be Sure You Get Enough Rest

"In six days you should do your work, and on the seventh day you must rest, so that your ox and your donkey may rest, and so that your son and your other helpers may be refreshed."

—Exodus 23:12

"See, the Lord has given you the sabbath. Therefore he gives you on the sixth day the bread of two days. Every man should abide in his place; let no man go out of his place on the seventh day."

So the people rested on the seventh day.

—Exodus 16:29-30

And the work of righteousness will be peace, and the effect of righteousness will be quietness and assurance forever.

And my people will dwell in a peaceable habitation, in sure dwellings, and in quiet resting places.

—Isaiah 32:17-18

My flesh and my heart may fail, but God is the strength of my heart and my portion forever.
—Psalm 73:26

I laid down and slept; I awaked, for the Lord sustained me.

—Psalm 3:5

The apostles gathered around Jesus and reported to Him all that they had done and taught.

He said to them, "Come away by yourselves to a remote place and rest a little." For many people were coming and going, and they did not even have time to eat.

So they went away in the boat by themselves to a remote place.

—Mark 6:30-32

As Jesus got into the boat, His disciples followed Him. Suddenly, a violent storm arose on the sea, so that the boat was being swamped by the waves. But He was sleeping.

—Matthew 8:23-24

Watch What You Eat

There is nothing better for man than to eat and to drink, and that he experiences good in his toil. Indeed, this I have seen is from the hand of God.

—Ecclesiastes 2:24

Moreover, every man that eats and drinks and experiences good in all his toil; this is the gift of God.

—Ecclesiastes 3:13

Behold, this is what I have seen to be good: that it is appropriate to eat and to drink and to experience good in all one's labor which he toils for under the sun the few days of his life that God gave to him, for that is his portion.

Indeed, to every man that God has given riches and wealth and has empowered him to eat from it and to take his portion and to find joy in his toil, this is the gift of God.

—Ecclesiastes 5:18-19

"Therefore I urge you to take some food, for this is in anticipation of your safety, since not a hair from the head of any of you will perish."

So after he said these things and had taken some bread, he gave thanks to God in the presence of them all. And when he had broken it, he began to eat.

Then they all became cheerful, and they themselves took food as well.

—Acts 27:34-36

Therefore, whether you eat or drink or whatever you do, do all for God's glory.

—1 Corinthians 10:31

Don't Even Think about Drinking and Drugs

Do not associate with people who are heavy drinkers of wine, or with those who glut themselves on meat.

—Proverbs 23:20

Who has woes? Who has grief? Who has conflicts? Who has complaints? Who has wounds for no reason? Who has red eyes?

They belong to those who tarry over wine, and to those who are on the look-out for strong drink!

Do not gaze at wine because it glows red, because it makes a sparkle in a cup or because it goes down smoothly.

In the end it bites like a snake and wounds like an adder.

Your eyes will see strange things and your heart will speak absurdities.

You will be like someone who lies down in the middle of the ocean or who lies down at the top of a mast.

"They struck me, but I feel no pain! They hit me, but I did not know it! Whenever I wake up I will look for some more!"

—Proverbs 23:29-35

So make up your mind, be determined, be sober, and hope to the end for the grace that is to be brought unto you at the revelation of Jesus Christ.

—1 Peter 1:13

And don't get drunk with wine, which is recklessness, but be filled with the Spirit.

—Ephesians 5:18

Wine is a mocker, and strong drink makes an uproar. Anyone who goes astray in this way is not wise.

—Proverbs 20:1

But they also have sinned with wine, and through strong drink they are out of the way. The priest and the prophet have sinned with strong drink. They are swallowed up of wine. They are out of the way through strong drink. They make mistakes in vision; they stumble in judgment.

For all tables are full of vomit and filthiness, so that there is no place that is clean.

—Isaiah 28:7-8

GIVE IT ALL YOU'VE GOT

Go to the ant, loafer! Look at its ways and learn!

It has no leader, commander, or ruler, but it prepares its provisions in the summer. It gathers its food during the harvest.

How long, sluggard, will you stay in bed? When will you get up from your sleep?

—Proverbs 6:6-9

The ants are not a strong people, but they insure their food supply during summer.

The badgers are not a mighty people, but they set their homes in rocky crags.

Locusts have no king, but they all go out in good order.

Lizards—you can catch them in your hands, but they live in kings' palaces.

—Proverbs 30:25-28

Whoever works his land will have plenty to eat,
but whoever pursues idle fantasies is senseless.
—Proverbs 12:1

The hands of the diligent will rule, but laziness will turn into forced labor.

—Proverbs 12:24

Pay close attention to the condition of your flock. Give due regard to your herds.

For riches are not forever—even a crown is not for all time.

—Proverbs 27:23-24

"I have not coveted anyone's silver or gold or clothing.

"You yourselves know that these hands have provided for my needs and for those who were with me."

—Acts 20:33-34

For this reason, I endure all things because of the elect, so that they also may obtain the salvation which is in Christ Jesus, with eternal glory.

—2 Timothy 2:10

Strengthen Your Spiritual Life, Too

For while the training of the body has limited benefit, godliness is profitable for all things, since it holds promise not only for this life but for that which is to come.

—1 Timothy 4:8

These have indeed an appearance of wisdom in promoting self-imposed piety, humility, and severe treatment of the body, but they are of no value in checking fleshly indulgence.

—Colossians 2:23

On the last and most important day of the festival, Jesus stood up and cried out, "If anyone is thirsty, he should come to Me and drink!"

—John 7:37

Trust in the Lord and do good. In this way you will dwell in the land and you will be truly fed.

Delight yourself also in the Lord, and He will give you the desires of your heart.

—Psalm 37:3-4

The Lord is near to all those who call on Him, to all that call on Him in truth.

He will fulfill the desire of those who fear Him. He also will hear their cry and will save them.

—Psalm 145:18-19

And those who know Your name will put their trust in You, for You, Lord, have not forsaken those who seek You.

—Psalm 9:10

Keep Your Main Goal in Mind

In the meantime the disciples kept urging Him, "Rabbi, eat something."

But He said, "I have food to eat that you don't know about."

The disciples said to one another, "Could someone have brought Him something to eat?"

"My food is to do the will of Him who sent Me and to finish His work," Jesus told them.

—John 4:31-34

For surely those who are far from You will perish. You have destroyed all those who go wandering away from You.

But it is good for me to draw near to God. I have put my trust in the Lord God, that I may declare all Your works.

—Psalm 73:27-28

Therefore if anyone is in Christ, there is a new creation. Old things have passed away, and look—they have become new.

Now everything is from God, who reconciled us to Himself through Christ and gave to us the ministry of reconciliation—that is, God was in Christ reconciling the world to Himself, not counting their offenses against them, and has committed to us the message of reconciliation.

Therefore, we are ambassadors for Christ, as though God were appealing through us. We plead on Christ's behalf: "Be reconciled to God."

—2 Corinthians 5:17-20

"Go, therefore, and make disciples of all nations, baptizing them in the name of the Father and of the Son and of the Holy Spirit, teaching them to observe everything I have commanded you. And remember, I am with you always, to the end of the age."

—Matthew 28:19-20

Check It Out . . .

Discipline is rarely pretty in the middle of it, but it yields results that you get no other way.

Jephthah—When a man can't control himself, he can hurt a lot of people. (Judges 11:29-40)

Ezra—Whether in the pouring rain or a boring work-room, he still stayed on task. (Ezra 10:9-17)

Virtuous Woman—There's a lot to be said for her hard work and dedication. (Proverbs 31:10-31)

Daniel—He had his choice at the king's table, but he knew what was good for him. (Daniel 1:3-16)

Luke—The good doctor worked overtime as a writer so he could tell Jesus' story. (Luke 1:1-4)

Faith

Everything which has been born of God conquers the world. And this is the victory which has conquered the world: our faith.

—1 JOHN 5:4

"These guys are skating like they think we can't win a game all season," Justin said. "But look, we're not that bad a hockey team!"

I looked around at the other players practicing their slap shots. Some of the guys were mouthing off. Others were just goofing off. It didn't look too promising.

Last year was the pits.
Could we sink any lower?

"Tell you what," I said. "It's up to us. We gotta lead these guys. We're the ones to pump 'em up a little."

"You got it, man!" Justin said. "If we don't do it, who will?"

Get Pumped!

Beloved ones, making all haste to write to you about our common salvation, I needed to write to you exhorting you to strive earnestly for the faith once delivered to the saints.

—Jude 1:3b

Do not lack diligence; be fervent in spirit; serve the Lord.

—Romans 12:11b

For the zeal of Your house has eaten me up.

—Psalm 69:9a

Don't Let Doubt Pull You Down

"If I had called and He had answered me, I would not believe that He had heard my voice.

"For he breaks me with a tempest and multiplies my wounds without cause.

"He will not allow me to take my breath, but fills me with bitterness.

"If I speak of strength, surely He is strong; and if I speak of judgment, who will set me a time to plead?

"If I justify myself, my own mouth will condemn me; if I say, 'I am perfect,' it will also prove me perverse.

"Though I were perfect, yet I would not know my soul. I would despise my life."

—Job 9:16-21

"Therefore I am troubled at His presence; when I consider, I am afraid of Him.

"For God makes my heart soft, and the Almighty troubles me.

"Because I was not cut off before the darkness, He has not covered the darkness from my face."

—Job 23:15-17

Truly I have cleansed my heart in vain, and washed my hands in innocency.

For all the day long I have been plagued, and chastened every morning.

If I say, "I will speak like this," behold, I would offend the generation of Your children.

When I thought to know this, it was too painful for me, until I went into the sanctuary of God. Then I understood their end.

—Psalm 73:13-17

"Come!" Jesus said. And climbing out of the boat, Peter started walking on the water and came toward Jesus.

But when he saw the strength of the wind, he was afraid. And beginning to sink, he cried out, "Lord, save me!"

Immediately, Jesus reached out His hand, caught hold of him, and said to him, "You of little faith, why did you doubt?"

—Matthew 14:29-31

Then Jesus said to him, " 'If You can?' Everything is possible to the one who believes."

Immediately the father of the boy cried out, "I do believe! Help my unbelief."

—Mark 9:23-24

When Pharaoh drew near, the children of Israel lifted up their eyes and, behold, the Egyptians marched after them. And they were terribly afraid, and the children of

Israel cried out to the Lord.

They said to Moses, "Because there were no graves in Egypt, is that why you have taken us away to die in the wilderness? Why have you dealt with us like this, to carry us forth out of Egypt?

"Isn't the word true that we told you in Egypt when we said, 'Let us alone that we may serve the Egyptians'? For it would have been better for us to serve the Egyptians than to die in the wilderness."

And Moses said to the people, "Do not be afraid. Stand still and see the salvation of the Lord, which He will show to you today, for you will not see the Egyptians whom you have seen today anymore forever.

"The Lord will fight for you, and you will hold your peace."

—Exodus 14:10-14

"Be still, and know that I am God. I will be exalted among the heathen. I will be exalted in the earth."

—Psalm 46:10

Get to Know Your Heavenly Father

Who is a God like You who takes away iniquity, who passes over the rebellion of the remnant of his inheritance? He does not stubbornly hold in His anger forever, because he delights in steadfast covenant love.

He will repeatedly have compassion on us and tread on our iniquities. He will even cast all our sins into the depths of the sea.

—Micah 7:18-19

"The God who made the world and everything in it, since He is Lord of heaven and earth, does not live in shrines made by hands.

"Neither is He served by human hands, as though He needed anything, since He Himself gives to all, life and breath and everything.

"And He has made from one man every nation of men to live all over the face of the earth, and has determined the times prescribed for them and the boundaries of their habitats, so that they might seek God, if perhaps they might reach out for Him and find Him, even though He is not far from each one of us."

—Acts 17:24-27

For You are not a God who takes pleasure in wickedness; evil will not dwell with You.

The foolish will not stand in Your sight; You hate all workers of iniquity.

You will destroy those who speak lies; the Lord will abhor the bloody and deceitful man.

But as for me, I will come into Your house in the multitude of Your mercy; fearing You, I will worship toward Your holy temple.

—Psalm 5:4-7

Blessed be the Lord, who daily loads us with benefits—even the God of our salvation.

—Psalm 68:19

LISTEN WELL TO HIS WORD

I have hidden Your word in my heart, that I might not sin against You.

—Psalm 119:11

I will delight myself in Your statutes. I will not forget Your word.

—Psalm 119:16

Then I will have an answer for him who reproaches me, for I trust in Your word.

—Psalm 119:42

Remember the word to Your servant, upon which you have caused me to hope.

This is my comfort in my affliction, for Your word has quickened me.

—Psalm 119:49-50

Give ear, O my people, to my law. Incline your ears to the words of my mouth.

I will open my mouth in a parable. I will utter dark sayings of old, which we have heard and known, which our fathers have told us.

We will not hide them from their children, showing to the generation to come the praises of the Lord—His strength and the wonderful works that He has done.

For He established a testimony in Jacob and appointed a law in Israel, which He commanded our fathers to make known to their children—that the generation to come might know them, even the children yet to be born, who will likewise arise and declare them to their children.

—Psalm 78:1-6

My soul is continually in my hand, yet I do not forget Your law.

The wicked have laid a snare for me, yet I strayed not from Your precepts.

I have taken Your testimonies as a heritage forever, for they are the rejoicing of my heart.

I have inclined my heart to perform Your statutes always, even to the end.

—Psalm 119:109-112

All Scripture is God-breathed and is profitable for teaching, for rebuking, for correcting, for disciplining in righteousness, so that God's man may be capable and equipped for every good work.

—2 Timothy 3:16-17

For the Word of God is living and effective and sharper than any two-edged sword, penetrating to the division of soul and spirit, of joints and marrow, and is a judge of the thoughts and deliberations of the heart.

And there is not a creature invisible before Him, but all things are naked and revealed to the eyes of Him with whom we have to do.

—Hebrews 4:12-13

When in Doubt, Trust in God

"Behold, I am the Lord, the God of all flesh. Is there anything too hard for Me?"

—Jeremiah 32:27

"For nothing will be impossible with God."

—Luke 1:37

For we walk by faith, not by sight.

—2 Corinthians 5:7

But as for you, continue in the things you have learned and have firmly believed, knowing from whom you learned them.

And that from a child, you have known the sacred Scriptures, which are able to make you wise for salvation through faith in Christ Jesus.

—2 Timothy 3:14-15

But remember the former days, in which, after you had been enlightened, you endured a hard struggle of sufferings, partly by being publicly exposed to insult and tribulations, and partly by having become companions of those who were so treated.

For you both sympathized with those in prison, and welcomed with joy the confiscation of your belongings, knowing that you yourselves have a better and lasting possession there.

Don't throw away your confidence, which has a great reward.

—Hebrews 10:32-35

Now faith is the reality of things hoped for, the proof of things not seen.

For by it the elders gained God's approval.

—Hebrews 11:1-2

The steps of a good man are ordered by the Lord, and He delights in his way.

Though he falls, he will not be utterly cast down, for the Lord upholds him with His hand.

—Psalm 37:23-24

God Will Do What He Says

He said, "If you will diligently listen to the voice of the Lord your God, and will do that which is right in His sight, and will give ear to His commandments and keep all His statutes, I will put none of these diseases upon you which I have brought upon the Egyptians, for I am the Lord who heals you."

—Exodus 15:26

I have been young and now I am old, yet I have not seen the righteous forsaken or his children begging for bread.

—Psalm 37:25

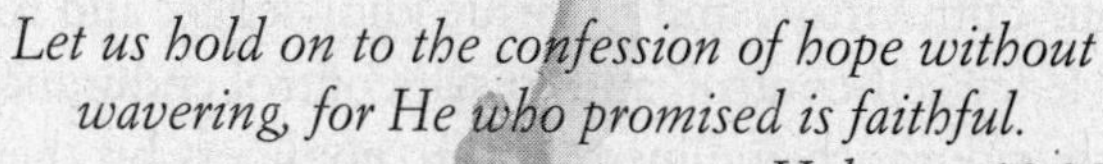

Let us hold on to the confession of hope without wavering, for He who promised is faithful.
—Hebrews 10:23

Without faith it is impossible to be pleasing to Him, for the one who draws near to God must believe that He exists and that He is a rewarder of those who seek Him.

—Hebrews 11:6

For you need endurance, so that after you have done the will of God, you may receive the promise: "For yet in a very little while, He who is coming will come and will not tarry."

—Hebrews 10:36-37

What then? If some did not believe, will their unbelief cancel God's faithfulness?

Absolutely not! God must be true and every man a liar, as it is written: "That You may be justified in Your words and triumph when You judge."

—Romans 3:3-4

Your Faith Will Pay off in the End

These very great and precious promises have been given to us, so that by them we may become partakers of the divine nature, having escaped from the corruption in the world because of lust.

Now for this very reason, exercising all diligence, add to your faith virtue, and to virtue knowledge, and to knowledge self-control, and to self-control endurance, and to endurance godliness, and to godliness brotherly kindness, and to brotherly kindness love.

For if these qualities are yours and abound, they render you neither unproductive nor unfruitful in the knowledge of our Lord Jesus Christ.

—2 Peter 1:4-8

For if dead people do not rise, Christ has not risen.

And if Christ has not risen, your faith is futile. You are still in your sins!

Consequently those who have gone to their rest in Christ have perished!

If it's only in this life we have set our hope on Christ, we are of all people the most to be pitied!

But now Christ has risen from the dead! He has become the firstfruits of those who have gone to their rest.

—1 Corinthians 15:16-20

"For I know that my redeemer lives, and that He will stand at the last day on the earth.

"And though worms will destroy this body after I die, yet in my flesh I will see God.

"I will see Him for myself. My eyes will behold Him and not another, though my heart is consumed within me."

—Job 19:25-27

Remember—Your Captain Is Coming Back

For it was fitting for Him for whom all things exist and through whom all things exist, when bringing many sons to glory, to perfect the pioneer of their salvation through sufferings.

—Hebrews 2:10

He will arbitrate between many nations and judge between strong and distant nations. So they will hammer their swords into hoes, even their spears into pruning knives. Nation will not fight against nation. They will never train for war again.

—Micah 4:3

For the land will be filled with the knowledge of the glory of the Lord, as the waters cover the sea.

—Habakkuk 2:14

" 'And I will shake all the nations, and the desire of all nations will come. And I will fill this house with glory,' says the Lord of hosts.

" 'The silver is Mine and the gold is Mine,' says the Lord of hosts.

" 'The glory of this final house will be greater than the former one,' says the Lord of hosts, 'and I will give peace in this place," says the Lord of hosts."

—Haggai 2:7-9

And in that day, living waters will go out from Jerusalem—half of them toward the eastern sea and half of them toward the western sea. It will be like this both in summer and in winter.

And the Lord will be king over all the earth. There will be only one Lord in that day, and He will have only one name.

—Zechariah 14:8-9

The Lord said unto my Lord, "Sit here at my right hand until I make Your enemies Your footstool."

—Psalm 110:1

Faith in Jesus Puts You on God's Side

Jesus, who is the outshining of God's glory and the exact imprint of His essence, and is sustaining all things by His Word of Power, after having made purification for sins, sat down at the right hand of the Majesty on high.

—Hebrews 1:3

Then the kings of the earth, the nobles, the military commanders, the rich, the powerful, and every slave and free person hid in the caves and among the rocks of the mountains.

And they said to the mountains and to the rocks, "Fall on us and hide us from the face of the One seated on the throne and from the wrath of the Lamb, because the great day of their wrath has come! And who is able to stand?"

—Revelation 6:15-17

"But who may abide the day of His coming, and who will stand when He appears? For He is like a refiner's fire and a launderer's soap.

"He will sit as a refiner and purifier of silver, and He will purify the sons of Levi and purge them as gold and silver, that they may offer to the Lord an offering in righteousness."

—Malachi 3:2-3

Then I saw a new heaven and a new earth, for the first heaven and the first earth had passed away, and the sea existed no longer.

I also saw the Holy City, new Jerusalem, coming down out of heaven from God, prepared like a bride adorned for her husband.

Then I heard a loud voice from the throne: "Look! God's dwelling is with men, and He will live with them. They will be His people, and God Himself will be with them and be their God."

—Revelation 21:1-3

Therefore, my beloved brothers, be steadfast, immovable, always overflowing in the Lord's work, because you know that, in the Lord, your labor is not for nothing.

—1 Corinthians 15:58

Check It Out . . .
Would it help you have more faith if you could read about others who had more faith?

Roman Centurion—The extent of his faith put God's own people to shame. (Matthew 8:5-13)

Zechariah & Elizabeth—A baby was coming that they'd been praying for a long time. (Luke 1:5-17)

Widow—She didn't stand much of a chance, but she had no chance if she said nothing. (Luke 18:1-8)

Thomas—They could believe it if they wanted, but he had to see it for himself. (John 20:24-29)

Ananias—Didn't God know that this Paul fellow killed people for less than this? (Acts 9:10-20)

Victory

But thanks be to God, who gives us the victory through our Lord Jesus Christ!

—1 Corinthians 15:57

One more out is all it takes for us to win—
or one more hit for them. The line between victory
and defeat can be pretty thin, especially in fast-pitch softball.
Heather unleashes her "fog ball," and the batter launches
a high floater deep to center. That's my territory!

One more out is all it takes.

I race back, my heart pounding.
Where's that fence? How close behind me?

I've got it pegged. I look. I wait. *Will it ever come down?*
Will I grab it? Will it hit my glove and pop out?

Phwaappp!
Oh, the sweet, sweet sound of victory!

THE THRILL OF VICTORY

Blessed are the people who know the joyful sound. They will walk, O Lord, in the light of Your countenance.

—Psalm 89:15

Sing, O you heavens, for the Lord has done it! Shout, you lower parts of the earth! Break forth into singing, you mountains, you forest, and every tree within, for the Lord has redeemed Jacob and glorified Himself in Israel.

—Isaiah 44:23

"You loved righteousness and hated lawlessness. Therefore, Your God anointed You with the oil of exultation beyond Your comrades."

—Hebrews 1:9

You have turned my mourning into dancing. You have put off my sackcloth and clothed me with gladness.

Because of this, I will sing praise to You and will not be silent. O Lord my God, I will give thanks to You forever.

—Psalm 30:11-12

Blessed be the Lord my strength, who teaches my hands to war and my fingers to fight.

He is my goodness, my fortress, my high tower, my deliverer, my shield, and the One in whom I trust—the One who subdues my people under me.

—Psalm 144:1-2

God Can Give You Winning Ways

"No weapon that is formed against you will prosper, and you will be able to condemn every tongue that rises against you in judgment. This is the heritage of the servants of the Lord, and their righteousness is from Me," says the Lord.

—Isaiah 54:17

The Lord is the portion of my inheritance and of my cup. He maintains my lot.

The lines have fallen for me in pleasant places. Yes, I have a goodly heritage.

—Psalm 16:5-6

Those who sow in tears will reap in joy.

He who goes out crying, bearing precious seed, will certainly come back again with rejoicing, bringing his harvest with him.

—Psalm 126:5-6

So Jesus told them this parable: "What man among you, who has a hundred sheep and loses one of them, does not leave the ninety-nine in the open field and go after the lost one until he finds it?

"When he has found it, he joyfully puts it on his shoulders, and coming home, he calls his friends and neighbors together, saying to them, 'Rejoice with me, because I have found my lost sheep!'

"I tell you, in the same way, there will be more joy in heaven over one sinner who repents than over ninety-nine righteous people who don't need repentance.

—Luke 15:3-7

It's OK to Celebrate

And as they came, when David had returned from the slaughter of the Philistine, that the women came out of all the cities of Israel, singing and dancing to meet king Saul with tabrets, with joy, and with instruments of music.

And the women answered one another as they played, and said, "Saul has killed his thousands and David his ten thousands."

—1 Samuel 18:6-7

And they came to Jerusalem with psalteries and harps and trumpets to the house of the Lord.

—2 Chronicles 20:28

O clap your hands, all you people! Shout to God with the voice of triumph!

For the Lord most high is terrible. He is a great King over all the earth.

He will subdue the people under us, and the nations under our feet.

He will choose our inheritance for us, the excellency of Jacob whom He loved.

God is gone up with a shout, the Lord with the sound of a trumpet.

Sing praises to God, sing praises! Sing praises to our

King, sing praises!

For God is the King of all the earth. Sing out praises with understanding.

God reigns over the heathen. God sits on the throne of His holiness.

The princes of the people are gathered together, even the people of the God of Abraham, for the shields of the earth belong to God. He is greatly exalted.

—Psalm 47:1-9

Cry out and shout, you inhabitants of Zion, for great is the Holy One of Israel in your midst.

—Isaiah 12:6

Enjoy it Now, But Tomorrow's Another Game

Stay alert. Stand fast in the faith. Be brave. Be strong.

—1 Corinthians 16:13

This command I am laying upon you, Timothy, my son, on the basis of the prophecies previously made concerning you, that you may by them fight the good fight, holding on to faith and a good conscience. By rejecting these, some have suffered the shipwreck of their faith.

—1 Timothy 1:18-19

So then, let's not sleep like the rest, but let's watch and be sober.

—1 Thessalonians 5:6

Plead my cause, O Lord, with those who strive with me. Fight against those who fight against me.

Take hold of shield and buckler, and stand up for my help.

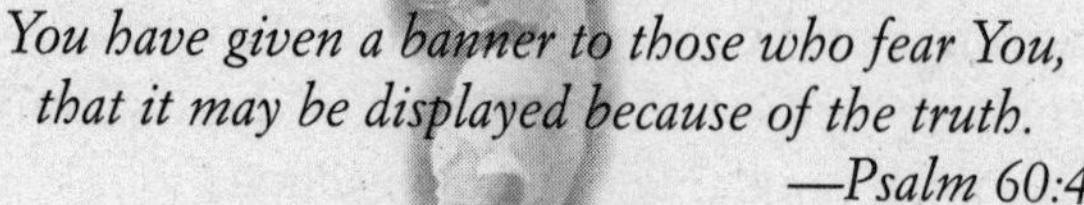

You have given a banner to those who fear You,
that it may be displayed because of the truth.
—Psalm 60:4

CUT OUT THE TRASH TALKING

"A good man produces good things from his storeroom of good, and an evil man produces evil things from his storeroom of evil.

"I tell you that on the day of judgment people will have to account for every careless word they speak.

"For by your words you will be acquitted, and by your words you will be condemned."

—Matthew 12:35-37

He was oppressed and He was afflicted, yet He did not open His mouth. He was brought as a lamb to the slaughter. And just like a sheep is quiet before her shearers, so He did not open His mouth.

—Isaiah 53:7

The scheme of a fool is sin. A mocker is an abomination to the human race.

—Proverbs 24:9

Proud, arrogant, and mocker are his names—anyone who behaves with conceited anger.

—Proverbs 21:24

Drive away the mocker so that conflict will depart, so that lawsuits and disgrace will cease.

—Proverbs 22:10

A mocker has no love for anyone who corrects him. He will not join the wise.

—Proverbs 15:12

Know this first, that in the last days scoffers will come in their mocking, who follow their own lusts.

—2 Peter 3:3

Now we who are strong have an obligation to help in the weaknesses of those without strength, and not to please ourselves.

Each one of us must please his neighbor for his good in order to build him up.

For even the Messiah did not please Himself. On the contrary, as it is written, "The insults of those who insult You have fallen on Me."

—Romans 15:1-3

It's God Who Gives the Victory

"Behold, the days come," says the Lord,"when I will raise unto David a righteous Branch, and a King will reign and prosper and will execute judgment and justice in the earth."

—Jeremiah 23:5

" 'Then the kingship and the dominion and the greatness of the kingdoms under the whole heaven will be given to the people, the saints of the Most High. His kingdom will be an everlasting kingdom, and all dominions will serve and obey Him.' "

—Daniel 7:27

"He will be great and will be called the Son of the Most High, and the Lord God will give Him the throne of His father David.

"He will reign over the house of Jacob forever, and His kingdom will have no end."

—Luke 1:32-33

For Christ did not enter a sanctuary made with human hands, but into heaven itself, now to appear before the face of God for us.

—Hebrews 9:24

Christ is gone into heaven and is on the right hand of God. Angels, authorities, and powers are all subject to him.

—1 Peter 3:22

They said with a loud voice: "The Lamb who was slaughtered is worthy to receive power and riches and wisdom and strength and honor and glory and blessing!"

I heard every creature in heaven, on earth, under the earth, on the sea, and everything in them say: "Blessing and honor and glory and dominion to the One seated on the throne, and to the Lamb, forever and ever!"

—Revelation 5:12-13

Now to the King eternal, immortal, invisible, to the only God who is, be honor and glory forever and ever. Amen.

—1 Timothy 1:17

Bow Down and Worship

Then I saw heaven opened, and there was a white horse! Its rider is called Faithful and True, and in righteousness He judges and makes war.

His eyes were like a fiery flame, and on His head were many crowns. He had a name written that no one knows except Himself.

—Revelation 19:11-12

Praise the Lord! Praise God in His sanctuary. Praise Him in the firmament of His power.

Praise Him for His mighty acts. Praise Him according to His excellent greatness.

Praise Him with the sound of the trumpet. Praise Him with the psaltery and harp.

Praise Him with the timbrel and dance. Praise Him with stringed instruments and organs.

Praise Him on the loud cymbals. Praise Him on the high sounding cymbals.

Let everything that has breath praise the Lord. Praise the Lord!

—Psalm 150:1-6

Praise the Lord! Praise the Lord, O my soul.
While I live, I will praise the Lord. I will sing praises to my God while I have my being.

—Psalm 146:1-2

For from Him and through Him and to Him are all things. To Him be the glory forever! Amen.

—Romans 11:36

God Offers Victory over All Your Enemies

O God the Lord, the strength of my salvation, You have covered my head in the day of battle.

—Psalm 140:7

"He teaches my hands to war, so that a bow of steel is broken by my arms."

—2 Samuel 22:35

Behold, all those who were incensed against You will be ashamed and confounded. They will be like nothing, and those who strive with You will perish.

—Isaiah 41:11

Wait on the Lord. Be of good courage, and He will strengthen your heart. Wait, I say, on the Lord.

—**Psalm 27:14**

Fight the good fight of faith. Lay hold on eternal life, into which you were called and made the good confession before many witnesses.

—**1 Timothy 6:12**

God Will Help You Defeat the Devil

"And I will put strife between you and the woman, and between your seed and her seed. It will bruise your head, and you will bruise his heel."

—**Genesis 3:15**

Therefore, submit to God. But stand up to the devil and he will flee from you.

—**James 4:7**

Now to whom you forgive anything, I also do it. In fact, if I have forgiven anything, what I forgive is because of you in the sight of Christ, in order that we might not be exploited by Satan. For we are not ignorant of his schemes.

—**2 Corinthians 2:10-11**

In Christ we were also made His inheritance, having been predestined according to the purpose of the One who works all things in agreement with the decision of His will, so that we will be to the praise of His glory (who first hoped in the Messiah).

—**Ephesians 1:11-12**

Be alert, be vigilant, because your enemy the devil walks around like a roaring lion, seeking whom he may devour.

Resist him strongly in the faith, knowing that the same afflictions are at work in your brothers who are in the world.

—1 Peter 5:8-9

God Will Give You Strength over Sin

For I do not understand what I am doing, because I do not practice what I want to do, but I do what I hate!

—Romans 7:15

For I do not do the good that I want to do, but I practice the evil that I do not want to do.

—Romans 7:19

For I joyfully agree with God's law in my inner self.

But I see a different law in the parts of my body, waging war against the law of my mind and taking me prisoner to the law of sin in the parts of my body.

—Romans 7:22-23

For the desire of the flesh is against the Spirit, while the desire of the Spirit is against the flesh. For these indeed are opposed to each other, so that you are not doing the things you would wish.

—Galatians 5:17

Dear friends, I plead with you as strangers and pilgrims: keep away from fleshly lusts, which war against the soul.

—1 Peter 2:11

For all those who are led by God's Spirit are God's sons.

—Romans 8:14

Victory Is Yours

My little children, I am writing you these things so that you may not sin. Yet if anyone does sin, we have an Advocate with the Father—Jesus Christ the righteous.

And He Himself is the sacrifice for our sins—yet not for ours only, but also for those of the whole world.

Now by this we know that we have come to know Him: If we keep His commands.

Whoever says, "I have come to know Him," and yet does not keep His commands is a liar, and the truth is not in that person.

—1 John 2:14

The God of peace will soon crush Satan under your feet.

—Romans 16:20a

He will swallow up death in victory, and the Lord God will wipe away tears from off all faces. He will take away the rebuke of His people from off all the earth, for the Lord has spoken it.

—Isaiah 25:8

Now when this perishable body is clothed with imperishability, and when this mortal body is clothed with immortality, then will take place what is written: "Death has been swallowed up in victory. O Death, where is your victory? O Death, where is your sting?"

—1 Corinthians 15:54-55

No, in all these things we are more than victorious through Him who loved us.

—Romans 8:37

VICTORY CAN BE YOUR WAY OF LIFE

" 'Anyone who has an ear should listen to what the Spirit says to the churches. I will give the victor the right to eat from the tree of life, which is in the paradise of God.' "

—Revelation 2:7

" 'Anyone who has an ear should listen to what the Spirit says to the churches. I will give the victor some of the hidden manna. I will also give him a white stone, and on the stone a new name is inscribed that no one knows except the one who receives it.' "

—Revelation 2:17

" 'In the same way, the victor will be dressed in white clothes, and I will never erase his name from the book of life, but will acknowledge his name before My Father and before His angels.' "

—Revelation 3:5

" 'The victor—I will make him a pillar in the sanctuary of My God, and he will never go out again. I will write on him the name of My God, and the name of the city of My God—the new Jerusalem, which comes down out of heaven from My God—and My new name.' "

—Revelation 3:12

" 'The victor—I will give him the right to sit with Me on My throne, just as I also won the victory and sat down with My Father on His throne.' "

—Revelation 3:21

"They conquered him by the blood of the Lamb and by the word of their testimony, for they did not love their lives in the face of death."

—Revelation 12:11

The Crown Awaits the Victor

" 'I am coming quickly. Hold on to what you have, so that no one takes your crown.' "

—Revelation 3:11

Finally, there is reserved for me the crown of righteousness, which the Lord, the righteous Judge, will give me on that day, and not to me only, but to all those who have loved His appearing.

—2 Timothy 4:8

But just as it is written: "The things that eye has not seen and ear has not heard—yes, it has not entered the heart of man, the things God has prepared for those who love Him!"

—1 Corinthians 2:9

For we know that if the earthly tent we live in is destroyed, we have a building from God, a house not made with hands, eternal in the heavens.

In fact in this one we groan, longing to put on our house which is from heaven, provided that when we are so clothed, we will not be found naked.

For while we are in this tent, we groan because we are burdened with it, not that we want to be unclothed, but to be clothed, so that mortality may be swallowed up by life.

And the One who prepared us for this very thing is God, who gave us the deposit of the Spirit.

Therefore we are always confident and know that while we are at home in the body we are away from the Lord.

—2 Corinthians 5:1-6

No One Can Take Away Your Prize

" 'For I know the thoughts that I think toward you,' says the Lord, 'thoughts of peace and not of evil, to give you an expected end.' "

—Jeremiah 29:11

But God who is abundant in mercy, because of His great love with which He loved us, even though we were dead in trespasses, made us alive with the Messiah—by grace you are saved!

He also raised us up with Him and seated us with Him in the heavenly places in Christ Jesus.

—Ephesians 2:4-6

"But My righteous one will live by faith; and if he draws back, my soul has no pleasure in him."

But we are not those who shrink back to destruction, but of faith to the preserving of the soul.

—Hebrews 10:38-39

On the contrary, you have come to Mount Zion and to the city of the living God, heavenly Jerusalem, and to myriads of angels in festive assembly.

—Hebrews 12:22

For we know in part and we prophesy in part.

But when that which is perfect has come, that which is will be done away.

When I was a child, I spoke as a child, I understood as a child, I thought as a child. When I became a man, I put away childish things.

For now we see in a mirror, dimly, but then face to face. Now I know in part, but then I will know just as I also am known.

—1 Corinthians 13:9-12

CHECK IT OUT . . .

The Bible's story is one of never-ending hope and lasting victory. Is it your story, too?

Miriam—The enemies laid dead at the bottom of the sea. Let's hear some cheering! (Exodus 15:11-21)

Deborah—God had won the victory. And this brave leader couldn't say it enough. (Judges 5:1-12)

Solomon—The temple was built and it looked beautiful. He was ready to celebrate! (1 Kings 8:1-14)

Rehoboam—He won the throne all right, but he didn't handle victory very well. (1 Kings 12:1-15)

Lazarus—He lived life the right way, and won the prize when others blew their shot. (Luke 16:19-26)

Champions

For in Him the whole fullness of God dwells bodily, and you have come to fullness in Him, who is the head of every ruler and authority.

—Colossians 2:9-10

I've improved my golf game just by hanging around the right guys. Like the pro at the city course.

He calls me over once and says: "Buddy, let me show you something. You're dipping your shoulders on your downswing, see? Take a look at the way I do it."

He creams a drive so low and deep, it looks like it's going to land in the next county. Way, way off, it starts to sorta rise a little, then just keeps floating, hanging, sailing toward the pin.

"You can make it go right or left, too," he says. "Just turn your wrist a little, like this. Watch me."

I still have a long way to go. It's a little-by-little thing, you know. But it helps to hang around a guy who knows how to do it right.

Because pretty soon, you're doing it right, too.

Who Do You Hang Out With?

When they observed the boldness of Peter and John and realized that they were uneducated and untrained men, they were amazed. Then they recognized them as having been with Jesus.

—**Acts 4:13**

Even for this you were called, because Christ also suffered for us, leaving us an example—that you should follow His steps.

—**1 Peter 2:21**

Get to Know This Champion Personally

In the beginning was the Word, and the Word was with God, and the Word was God.

He was with God in the beginning.

All things were created through Him, and apart from Him not one thing was created that has been created.

In Him was life, and that life was the light of men.

—**John 1:1-4**

He came to His own, and His own people did not receive Him.

But to all who did receive Him, He gave them the right to be children of God, to those who believe in His name, who were born, not of blood, or of the will of the flesh, or of the will of man, but of God.

The Word became flesh and took up residence among us. We observed His glory, the glory as the only Son from the Father, full of grace and truth.

—**John 1:11-14**

Our Sin Cost Him Dearly

And you know that He was revealed to take away our sins, and there is no sin in Him.

—1 John 3:5

Therefore, just as sin entered the world through one man, and death through sin, in this way death spread to all men, because all have sinned.

—Romans 5:12

For all have sinned and fall short of the glory of God.

—Romans 3:23

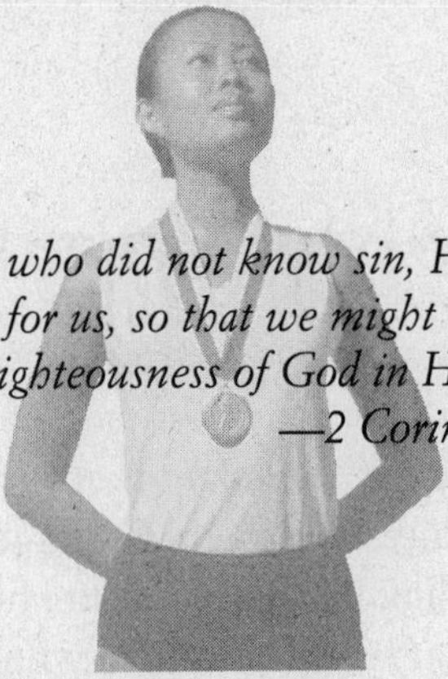

The One who did not know sin, He made Him sin for us, so that we might become the righteousness of God in Him.

—2 Corinthians 5:21

So then, as through one trespass there is condemnation for everyone, so also through one righteous act, there is life-giving justification for everyone.

For just as through one man's disobedience the many were made sinners, so also through the one man's obedience the many will be made righteous.

—Romans 5:18-19

He Has Given Us a Way Out

But God proves His own love for us in that while we were still sinners, Christ died for us!

—Romans 5:8

Jesus told him, "I am the way, the truth, and the life. No one comes to the Father except through Me."

—John 14:6

"I am the door. If anyone enters by Me, he will be saved, and will come in and go out and find pasture.

"A thief comes only to steal and to kill and to destroy. I have come that they may have life and have it in abundance."

—John 10:9-10

For through Him we both have access by one Spirit to the Father.

So therefore you are no longer foreigners and strangers, but fellow citizens with the saints and members of God's household, built on the foundation of the apostles and prophets—the cornerstone being Christ Jesus Himself.

The whole building is fit together in Him and grows into a holy sanctuary in the Lord, in whom you also are being built for God's dwelling in the Spirit.

—Ephesians 2:18-22

So Whatta You Say?

If we say that we have no sin, we are deceiving ourselves, and the truth is not in us.

If we confess our sins He is faithful and righteous so that He forgives us our sins and cleanses us from all unrighteousness.

—1 John 1:8-9

When I kept silent, my bones grew old through my roaring all the day long.

For day and night, Your hand was heavy on me. My moisture turned into the drought of summer.

I have acknowledged my sin to You, and I have not hidden my iniquity. I said, "I will confess my transgressions to the Lord," and You forgave the iniquity of my sin.

—Psalm 32:3-5

When they heard this, they were deeply troubled, and said to Peter and the rest of the apostles: "Men and brothers, what should we do?"

Then Peter said to them, "Repent and let each of you be baptized in the name of Jesus the Messiah for the forgiveness of your sins, and you will receive the gift of the Holy Spirit."

—Acts 2:37-38

If you confess with your mouth "Jesus is Lord," and believe in your heart that God raised Him from the dead, you will be saved.

With the heart one believes for righteousness, and with the mouth confession is made for salvation.

—Romans 10:9-10

For "everyone who calls on the name of the Lord will be saved."

—Romans 10:13

There's No Life Like the Christian Life

"One thing I do know: I was blind, and now I can see!"

—John 9:25b

Whom do I have in heaven but You? And there is no one on earth that I desire besides You.

—Psalm 73:25

This is eternal life: that they may know You, the only true God, and the One You have sent—Jesus Christ.

—John 17:3

But whatever things were gain to me, I have considered these things loss for Christ.

But more than that, I also consider all things to be loss because of the surpassing greatness of knowing Christ Jesus my Lord, on account of whom I have suffered the loss of all things and consider them dung so that I may gain Christ and be found in Him, not having my righteousness from the law, but through faith in Christ—the righteousness which is from God based on faith.

—Philippians 3:7-9

For you have died, and your life is hidden with Christ in God.

When Christ who is your life is revealed, then you also will be revealed with Him in glory.

—Colossians 3:3-4

Want God More Than You Want Anything

"If you love Me, you will keep My commandments."

—John 14:15

"Keep asking, and it will be given to you. Keep searching, and you will find. Keep knocking, and the door will be opened to you."

—Matthew 7:7

"Whatever you ask in My name, I will do it, so that the Father may be glorified in the Son.

"If you ask Me anything in My name, I will do it."

—John 14:13-14

I have no greater joy than this: that I hear my children are walking in the truth.

—3 John 1:4

Be a Champion in Real Life

And whatever you do, in word or deed, do everything in the name of the Lord Jesus, giving thanks to God the Father through Him.

—Colossians 3:17

"Therefore, everyone who acknowledges Me before men, I will also acknowledge Him before My Father in heaven.

"But whoever denies Me before men, I will also deny him before My Father in heaven."

—Matthew 10:32-33

Then He called a child to Him and had him stand among them.

"I assure you," He said, "unless you are converted and become like children, you will never enter the kingdom of heaven.

"Therefore, whoever humbles himself like this child—this one is the greatest in the kingdom of heaven."

—Matthew 18:2-4

Therefore let us go to Him outside the camp bearing his reproach, for we do not have here on earth an enduring city, but we intently seek one to come.

Through Him therefore, let us keep offering up a sacrifice of praise to God, the fruit of our lips that confess His name.

—Hebrews 13:13-15

Tell Someone What Jesus Has Done for You

Sing to the Lord; bless his name; show forth His salvation from day to day.

—Psalm 96:2

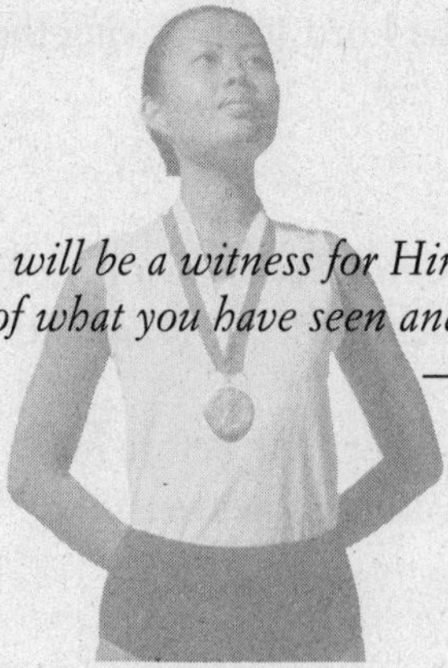

"For you will be a witness for Him to all mankind of what you have seen and heard."
—Acts 22:15

Let all those who seek You rejoice and be glad in You. Let those who love Your salvation say continually, "The Lord be magnified."

—Psalm 40:16

I will extol You, O Lord, for You have lifted me up and have not made my foes to rejoice over me.

O Lord my God, I cried to You, and You have healed me.

O Lord, You have brought up my soul from the grave.

You have kept me alive that I should not go down to the pit.

Sing unto the Lord, O you saints of His, and give thanks at the remembrance of His holiness. For His anger endures for only a moment. In His favor is life. Weeping may last for a night, but joy comes in the morning.

—Psalm 30:1-5

And in that day you will say, "Praise the Lord, call on His name, declare His doings among the people, make mention that His name is exalted.

"Sing to the Lord, for He has done excellent things. This is known in all the earth."

—Isaiah 12:4-5

As Jesus was getting into the boat, the man who had been demon-possessed kept begging Him to be with Him.

But He would not let him; instead, He told him, "Go back home to your own people, and report to them how much the Lord has done for you and how He has had mercy on you."

—Mark 5:18-19

You were made rich in everything by Him in all speaking and all knowledge, just as the testimony of Christ was made firm in you.

—1 Corinthians 1:5-6

Somebody Say "Praise the Lord"

"Then you will delight yourself in the Lord, and I will cause you to ride on the high places of the earth, and I will feed you with the heritage of Jacob your father, for the mouth of the Lord has spoken it."

—Isaiah 58:14

*Who will separate us from the love of Christ?
Will affliction or anguish or persecution or
famine or nakedness or danger or sword?*
—Romans 8:35

For I am persuaded that neither death nor life, nor angels nor rulers, nor things present, nor things to come, nor powers, nor height, nor depth, nor any other created thing will have the power to separate us from the love of God that is in Christ Jesus our Lord!

—Romans 8:38-39

"Yours, O Lord, are the greatness, the power, and the glory, the splendor, and the majesty; for everything in the heavens and on earth belongs to You. Yours, O Lord, is the kingdom, and You are exalted as head over all.

"Riches and honor come from You, and You are the ruler of everything. In Your hand are strength and might, and it is in Your hand to make great and to give strength to all.

"And now, our God, we give You thanks and praise Your glorious name."

—1 Chronicles 29:11-13

Check It Out . . .

We have a long list of champions in our heritage. And One who can take us through the finals.

Noah—Everybody told him he was crazy. You don't hear anybody saying it now. (Genesis 8:1-22)

Caleb—All the wimps were dead and gone, but Caleb was still itching for a fight. (Joshua 14:6-14)

Samuel—After all these years, he could stand and say he gave it everything he had. (1 Samuel 12:1-5)

Mary & Joseph—Faced with an impossible task, they trusted in God's Word. (Matthew 1:18-25)

Jesus—The only real champions are those who pin their hopes on Jesus Christ. (Revelation 22:16-21)

YOUR FAVORITE BIBLE PROMISES FOR CHAMPIONS

Your Favorite Bible Promises for Champions

YOUR FAVORITE BIBLE PROMISES FOR CHAMPIONS

Your Favorite Bible Promises for Champions

Your Favorite Bible Promises for Champions

Your Favorite Bible Promises for Champions

Author

Gary Wilde, a graduate of Bethany Seminary, has been a prolific free-lance writer and editor for Christian publishers since 1989. A former staff editor of trade books at David C. Cook, he now edits *The Quiet Hour* and also served as senior copy editor for *Christianity Today's* "Leadership Handbooks of Practical Theology."